Anonymous

Irenicum:

Or, the Importance of Unity in the Church of Christ Considered

Anonymous

Irenicum:
Or, the Importance of Unity in the Church of Christ Considered

ISBN/EAN: 9783337007577

Printed in Europe, USA, Canada, Australia, Japan

Cover: Foto ©Lupo / pixelio.de

More available books at **www.hansebooks.com**

IRENICUM:

OR,

THE IMPORTANCE OF

UNITY

IN THE

CHURCH OF CHRIST

CONSIDERED;

AND APPLIED TOWARDS THE HEALING
OF OUR
UNHAPPY DIFFERENCES AND DIVISIONS.

Ενδυσωμεθα την ὁμονοιαν, ταπεινοφρονυντες.
Clem. Epiſt. ad Corinth. ſect. 30.

LONDON:

Printed for J. and F. RIVINGTON, in St. Paul's Church-yard;
T. PAYNE, at the Meuſe Gate; and B. WHITE, in Fleet-ſtreet.

MDCCLXXV.

Importance *of* Unity, *&c.*

THE feafonablenefs of a difcourfe on this fubject muft appear at firft fight to every one, who pays the leaft regard, or attention to the religious differences which prevail among us; or who is at all verfed in the controverfy about fubfcription to the articles of the church of *England*; efpecially when it is confidered, that throughout the whole courfe of it, at leaft as far as it hath come in my way to be acquainted with it, very little notice feems to have been taken of the great principle of *unity* on the one fide, any more than on the other; which yet, it is humbly prefumed, ought to have

had

had the firſt place in the conſideration of both.

To recall the attention of all parties to this great and neceſſary point, was the ſole motive which overcame my reluctance to enter into this controverſy: Nor, indeed, could I ſcarce have prevailed with myſelf to intermeddle with it at all, had not this, and the other topicks, which I mean to dwell chiefly upon, been of a catholick and conciliating nature. Whence I wiſh to appear in the light of a moderator in this diſpute, who is deſirous of contributing his endeavours to heal our breaches, rather than to keep up the ball of contention, which hath been bandied about too much already.

Biſhop *Stillingfleet* publiſhed his *Irenicum* with the benevolent view of accommodating the differences between the church of *England,* and the Diſſenters of his time. Ambitious of following the ſteps of a prelate, who was ſo great an ornament to this church and nation, though *non paſſibus æquis,* I have taken the liberty of adopting the

the fame title, and prefixing it to a tract, the defign of which is of the fame nature, however deficient it may prove in the execution, and how far fhort foever it may fall of obtaining its end.

What is here offered for this purpofe confifts chiefly of obfervations on the following heads:

That the church of Chrift is founded upon *unity*—That this principle was carefully cultivated, and religioufly maintained, by the primitive church—That an early regard was paid to it by the church of *England* at the Reformation—That not only all the other Proteftant churches, and all the foreign divines of that age, but even the old non-conformifts here in *England*, had a deep fenfe of the importance of unity; ftrongly remonftrated againft fchifin; and condemned it as a great fin and heinous tranfgreffion.

Subfcription to the articles of faith required by the church of *England*, in order to preferve the unity of it, having been much controverted of late, the right,

wifdom,

wifdom, and utility, of fuch requifition is in the next place difcuffed and ftated; feveral queftions, arifing from this fubject, are incidentally refolved; and fome other expedients, which have been propofed, inftead of fubfcription to the *Thirty-nine articles,* as better anfwering the fame end, are impartially weighed and confidered.

The whole is clofed with an earneft exhortation to Chriftians of all denominations amongft us, to cultivate catholick and uniting principles, for the fake of promoting, and *endeavouring to keep the unity of the Spirit in the bond of peace.*

Firft, I defire it may be obferved, that the church of Chrift is founded upon *unity.*

This is one of the main pillars on which it refts; and this is implied in the very defign, nature, and tendency, of the Chriftian religion.

Unity of defign, and a confiftence and fymmetry of parts, is neceffary to the duration and ftability of every conftitution: And the Divine Founder of his church

knew

knew this fo well, that he lays it down as a certain truth, that *a houfe divided againft itfelf cannot ftand.*. And yet this great truth, fo obvious in itfelf, is at pre-fent fo little regarded, that we feem in a manner to have loft all fight of it. I therefore beg leave to infift a little more largely on a fubject that concerns the very effence of Chriftianity.

Our bleffed Lord died, that he might *gather together in one the children of God, that were fcattered abroad*[a], that there might *be one fold, and one fhepherd*[b],—that *they all might be one, as He and the Father are one, He in them, and they in him, that they might be made perfect in one*[c].

This implies the moft abfolute, com-plete, and finifhed union that can be con-ceived. In this his laft and longeft prayer to the Father, Chrift repeats his defire in five or fix different expreffions, that his difciples might be one, and kept in one body; which fhews how neceffary a part

[a] John, ch. xi. 51, 52. [b] Ch. x. 16.
[c] Ch. xvii. 22, 23.

B 3 of

of religion he intended this should be; and likewise intimates to us the danger he foresaw of his followers departing from it, which made him intercede so earnestly for it. And how entire and tender he meant to render this union, appears from his praying it might be such as that between the Father and himself was.

Every institution and appointment of our Lord manifested his intention of associating his followers into *one body.* He delivered his prayer to them all in the *plural,* to shew that he chiefly intended they should use it in a *body.* He appointed *baptism,* as the way of receiving men into this *body;* and the *eucharist,* as a joint memorial that the *body* of his disciples was to keep up of his death [d].

For the constant and perpetual maintenance of this spiritual connection, Christ hath, for his part, promised to be with his faithful disciples *always, unto the end of the world* [e]; and, to encourage them to asso-

[d] See Bishop *Burnett* on the Articles. Art. **XXXIV.**
[e] Matt. xxviii. 20.

ciate

ciate, and affemble together, for the continuance and improvement of it, in the feveral acts and ordinances of religious worfhip, and mutual good offices, which have a powerful tendency and influence in promoting love and harmony among Chriftians, he affures them, that where but *two or three are gathered together in his name, there he is in the midft of them*[f]. For the better effecting and ftrengthening this bleffed union among Chriftians, he confiders himfelf as their head, and the whole fociety, which he wills them to form, as his body, and members in particular, every one of them, of him, and of each other.

" The apoftles frequently ufe the figure " of a *body* to exprefs this union; than " which nothing can be imagined that is " more firmly knit together, and in which " all the parts do more tenderly fympa- " thize with one another[s]." And, to convince us of the perfect harmony to

[f] Matt. xviii. 20. [s] Bifhop *Burnet* ib.

which

which Chrift means to bring this his my-
ftical body the church, and in what juft
proportion and fymmetry of parts he
would have it all to be framed together,
however defective of this it may be at prefent ; the apoftle *Paul* compares it to the
human body, all the members of it acting
in conjunction with, and fubordination to,
each other, contributing to the fupport of
the whole, and being fo tempered together,
that there be no fchifm in the one, any
more than in the other ; but that all
*the members fhould have the fame care one
of another,* and fympathize with each
other [h].

I befeech you, brethren, faith the apoftle, in
this fame epiftle (for brethren we all are),
by the name of our Lord Jefus Chrift, of
whom the whole family in heaven and
earth is named, *that ye all fpeak the fame
thing,* and profefs the fame doctrine, *that
there be no divifions,* fchifms, *nor contentions,
among you:* but *that ye be perfectly joined,*
and framed together into one entire body,

[h] 1 Cor. xii.

in

*in the fame mind, and in the fame judge-
ment* [i], united in affection, and, as far as
poffible, in fentiment, belief, and principle likewife.

Agreeably to this, he elfewhere exhorts
us, *to endeavour*, with all our power, *to keep
the unity of the Spirit*, this fpiritual unity,
in the bond of peace, from the following
confiderations :—That the church of Chrift
is in its nature but *one, one* in its feveral
parts, and *one* likewife in the feveral perfons who govern and conftitute the whole
of it. *There is*, fays he, *one body, and one
fpirit*, or foul, which animates it, *even as
ye are called in one hope of your calling : One
Lord, one faith, one baptifm : One God, and
Father of all, who is above all, and through
all, and in you all* [k].

In order to promote and eftablifh this
perfect union, Chrift hath appointed feveral diftinct orders of men in his church;
for the due conduct and government of
it; the inftruction and difcipline of its
members; the keeping of them in a body;

---

[i] 1 Cor. i. 10, 11.   [k] Eph. iv. 3—6.

and

and for the better and more orderly admi-
niftration of its fervice and worfhip in its
feveral parts ; *for the perfecting,* or knitting
together, *of the faints* ; for the work *of the
miniftry* ; *for the edifying of the body of
Chrift* ; *till we all meet in the unity of the
faith* ; or arrive at an unity of faith, and
of the knowledge, or acknowledgement, *of
the Son of God, and grow up unto a perfect
man* ; as if we all were but as one perfon,
infpired with one foul ; and till we attain
unto *the meafure of* that *ftature* which is to
make up *the fullnefs of Chrift* :—That,
having obtained fuch a firmnefs of conftitution, we fhall then be no longer *toffed
to and fro like children, and carried about
with every wind of doctrine, by the fleight
and cunning craftinefs of men, according to
the fubtile method of impofture* [1] ; but, *fin-
cerely loving the truth, we fhall,* by that
means, grow up into a firm union *in all
things with Chrift our head, from whom the
whole body, being compacted and nurtured,*

---

[1] Gr. προς την μεθοδειαν της πλανης, literally *the me-
thodifm of impofture* ; an unlucky appellation.

or cemented, *together, obtains increaſe from every connection contributing to it, according to the efficacious operation of every part, in its proportion, to the edifying of itſelf in love* [m].

In the original this is expreſſed in ſuch ſtrong and complicated terms, as ſeem deſigned to impreſs the complicated and compact nature of that union, which is inculcated by it, the more deeply upon our minds. I have attempted a tranſlation, as expreſſive as I could render it, of the ſenſe of the original; but our language wants nerves to expreſs the nervous import of it. The ſame ſentiment occurs in another epiſtle of this ſame apoſtle, in almoſt the ſame words; importing, that from Chriſt, the head, the whole body of his church, like the natural body, is nouriſhed and 'knit together in love, by the joints, or ſutures, and ligaments, with which he hath united and bound all its parts to each other; and by this means it

[m] Eph. iv. 12—16,

is enabled to thrive and profper, and *to in-creafe with the increafe of God*[n].

A body, thus clofely cemented toge-ther, muft of courfe acquire the found-nefs and ftability of the moft complete body politick. Our Divine Lawgiver, there-fore, advanced it into a kingdom, which, in its conftitution, government, and laws, is framed to collect and preferve the fe-veral members of it in all outward acts, and inward difpofitions, of mutual peace, fidelity, benevolence, and agreement in fentiment, as well as affection, far fuperior to, and in a manner diftinct from, all the kingdoms of this world. Whence the Lord of it might juftly fay, his *kingdom was not of this world*,—not founded on the fame narrow maxims of policy which the kingdoms of this world are generally built upon: And he no lefs truly verified his promife of building his church upon a rock.

The fubjects of this kingdom are ac-cordingly exhorted, and ftrictly enjoined,

[n] Col. ii. 19.

to do all good offices, not only to each other, but to all mankind, even their very enemies; and to cultivate charity and good-will towards all the world; ftill in conformity to, and in purfuance of, the fame great principle of unity on which it is founded.

On this principle too it was, that our Lord *brake that middle wall of partition* between *Jew and Gentile* which had kept them afunder, and *made both one, in one body, by his crofs,* having thereby *flain* that *enmity* which had been between them °. For preferving this bleffed union, the apoftle *Paul,* in conjunction with the other apoftles, as there are grounds to fuppofe, prefcribed rules of uniformity, and fuppreffed the contentions of men, by the cuftom of the churches of God, to which he required all to conform ᴾ. And he ordained the fame practice in all the churches ꟼ. And hence, by the way, the church of *England* is juftified in enacting

---

° Eph. ii. 14, 15, 16.   ᴾ 1 Cor. xi. 16.
ꟼ 1 Cor. iv. 17. — xiv. 33.

laws

laws of uniformity, as it follows the pattern set by the apoftles in that refpect.

From the foregoing paffages of fcripture, we fee what ftrefs it lays upon unity in the church of Chrift, and how warmly it preffes the prefervation of it; than which we need no better argument of its great importance and neceffity.

Of this we fhall be ftill farther convinced from what the word of God fays of divifions in the church.

Our bleffed Lord teaches no more than what neceffarily refults from the nature of things, as already obferved :—That *every kingdom divided againft itfelf is brought to defolation*; and that *a city, or houfe, divided againft itfelf, cannot ftand* [r]. *Now I befeech you, brethren,* fays the apoftle, *mark them which caufe divifions and offences, contrary to the doctrine* of unity *which ye have learned, and avoid them* [s]. Having been informed, that there were *contentions* among the *Corinthians*, he befeeches them, *as they were brethren, by the name of their*

[r] Matt. xii. 25.   [s] Rom. xvi. 17.

common

common Lord and mafter *Jefus Chrift,* that they would *all fpeak the fame thing,* that there might be *no divifions,* or *fchifms,* as it is in the margin, *among them.* He reproves them very fharply for ranging themfelves under different leaders, *every one faying, I am of Paul, and I of Apollos, and I of Cephas, and I of Chrift. Is Chrift divided? was Paul crucified for you? or were ye baptized into the name of Paul?* fays St. *Paul* himfelf [t]. He blames them for their carnal tempers, from there being envying, and ftrife, and divifions, or factions, among them. And he cenfures them again upon the fame account; and obferves, that their fchifms and divifions muft of courfe be productive of fects and herefies [u]. And in the next chapter he fhews at large, as obferved above, how God had tempered the body of his church together, and difpofed the feveral members of it in fuch harmony, that there fhould be no fchifm or divifion in it, any more

[t] 1 Cor. i. 10, 11, 12, 13. ch. iii. 3.
[u] 1 Cor. xi. 18.

than

than in the human body [w]; and, fhould it by any violence be maimed and lacerated, and its feveral parts be torn and difmembered from it, we all know how fatal that would be to it: And, whenever the like happens to the fpiritual body of Chrift, it cannot be lefs deftructive in proportion; and every partial divifion, that is made in it, weakens, and tends more or lefs to diffolve the union of it, wherein its great ftrength confifts. Therefore every fpecies and degree of contention and feparation in the church is to be lamented, as a mark of God's difpleafure, drawn down for the punifhment of the fins of its members.

In the church of the *Ifraelites*, the dreadful deftruction of *Corah* and his factious affociates is held forth as an example and warning, to all future generations, of the fin and danger of divifions in the divine worfhip; the Lord doing *a new thing*, by caufing the earth to cleave afunder, and fwallow up this rebellious crew, at their

[w] 1 Cor. xii. 24, 25.

very

very rife; to prevent the mifchievous effects of ftirring up any oppofition to a le-
gal eftablifhment in his church[x].

It was *for the fins of her prophets, and the
iniquities of her priefts,* that *the anger of the
Lord divided them, and that he no more regarded them*[y]. From the whole it appears, that Chrift hath formed his church
into one bleffed fociety, by certain *laws of
connection* and coherence; which if Chriftians would fubmit to be governed by,
and religioufly obferve, would be the moft
effectual and indiffoluble of all others
whatfoever.

This is what we have good grounds to
expect they will in the end be brought to,
when there will be but *one fold under one
fhepherd*; of which more hereafter. And
this fociety is framed and linked together
upon fo comprehenfive a plan, that it is
not confined to the bounds of this earth;
which only furnifhes colonies, to be received into the far more extenfive regions,
occupied by the church triumphant in

---

[x] Numb. xvi. throughout.   [y] Lam. iv. 13. 16.

C   heaven;

heaven; both being in communion, and having an intercourse with each other.

Pursuant to this plan; I proceed to observe,

- *Secondly,* That this great principle of unity was carefully cultivated, and religiously maintained, by the primitive church.

The very first thing that the disciples of our Lord did after his departure from them, and his ascension into heaven, was to form themselves into a small society; *continuing stedfastly in the apostles doctrine and fellowship*; having sold all their goods and possessions, and thrown them into one common stock, for their mutual support; employed in the constant exercise of family-devotion; and at the same time, with one accord, daily frequenting the publick worship in the temple.

Their unanimity and charity gained them respect and admiration, and rapidly increased their number. *Three thousand* souls were added to them in one day; which soon grew to *five thousand*; and still

the

the multitude of them that believed were of one heart, and of one foul: Neither faid any of them, that aught of the things which he poſſeſſed was his own; for they had all things common [z]. And their love of each other was ſo remarkable, that it became notorious even to a proverb; and was the envy of their heathen neighbours.

The firſt difference that aroſe in the church was immediately ſettled by the authority of an apoſtolical council; which ordained ſome things, among others of greater conſequence, to be obſerved by the Gentile converts, that might be looked upon as mere articles of peace; being in themſelves ſo uneſſential to Chriſtianity, that they were generally diſregarded ſoon after the age in which they had been enjoined [a].

We have very probable grounds to believe, that, beſides the holy ſcriptures, there was a ſymbol of faith delivered to the church by the apoſtles, and their diſ-

---

[z] Acts iv. 32. [a] Acts xv. 20.

ciples;

ciples; which was embraced, and ſtrictly adhered to, throughout the whole Chriſtian world; and that this, for ſubſtance, was much the ſame with, what is now called, the apoſtles creed. This was *that form of doctrine, which was delivered to the church* [b];—That *form of ſound words*, which St. *Paul* charged *Timothy* to *hold faſt*;—That *good thing*, which, *by the grace of God's Spirit, he was to keep* [c];—*The things, which he had heard of him among many witneſſes; which he was to commit to faithful men, who ſhould be able to teach others alſo* [d];—*The things*, which he *had learned, and had been aſſured of, knowing of whom he had learned them* [e];—*The firſt principles of the oracles of God, and of the doctrine of Chriſt* [f]. This, in a word, was the ſame *faith* ſtill, which was *once delivered to the ſaints;* and which they were exhorted *earneſtly to contend for* [g].

---

[b] Rom. vi. 17.   [c] 2 Tim. i. 13, 14.
[d] 2 Tim. ii. 2.   [e] Ch. iii. 14.
[f] Heb. v. 12.—vi. 1.   [g] Jude 3.

All

All thefe different modes of expreffion agree in one and the fame import ; that if there was not fome certain ftandard, or fixed formulary of faith, delivered by the apoftles, and other planters of churches, to which all doctrines were to be reduced; yet that there were in all churches fuch forms as agreed in effentials, and were in fubftance the fame throughout.   Thefe were preferved with the greateft regard and veneration; and were chiefly committed to the care of the refpective bifhops, who were extremely watchful over their facred *depofitum* ; often meeting, and fometimes at the peril of their lives, to confult about the good of the church ; to preferve it, as far as they were able, in the true faith ; to prevent innovations, or to remonftrate againft them ; and at other times, fending profeffions of faith to each other, upon their agreement in which they held communion together.   And when any, either of the clergy or laity, removed, or traveled from one diocefe to another, they were furnifhed, by the

bifhop

bifhop of the diocefe, to which they be-
longed, with commendatory epiftles, mentioned by St. *Paul*[h]; in teftimony of love
and unity, and of the foundnefs and or-
thodoxy of their faith.

. Difputes indeed, and diffentions, arofe
in particular churches, even in the apoftolical age; but they were not carried fo
far, as to be productive of any formal, or
open fchifms; nor did they difturb the
peace of other churches: But there continued a general harmony and unanimity,
throughout the churches of the whole
world, during the three firft centuries,
not only in doctrine; but, for the moft
part, in their religious rites and obfer-
vances likewife.

. A difference in the obfervation of a day
was reckoned fo unhappy a thing, that
apoftolical practice and ufage, alledged on
both fides, was fcarce thought fufficient
to juftify the one half of the church, or
the other. And the difpute between the
Eaftern and Weftern churches, about

[h] 2 Cor. iii. 1.

keeping

keeping *Eafter*; was thought of fuch importance, as to require the authority of a general council to fettle it.

As different opinions arofe in the church, endeavours were conftantly ufed to adjuft them ; and, as herefies fprang up, councils, fome of which were general, were fummoned to cenfure and fupprefs, or to guard againft them. To this end *Creeds* came to be framed, enlarged, and multiplied; that the body of Chriftians might know what to believe and profefs, and be provided with antidotes againft falfe doctrines : All which proceeded from this general principle, namely, the neceffity of maintaining the unity of the catholick faith, and of preferving it whole and undefiled.

Schifms and divifions in the church were looked upon as of the moft deplorable and dangerous confequence ; and thofe that caufed them were anathematized, and avoided, as the pefts of fociety. St. *Cyprian* laments fchifm as the greateft evil that can befal the church, and

reckons

reckons it to be a crime of so deep a
die, as not to be expiated even by martyr-
dom[1]. When any diffentions or difputes
arofe, to difturb the peace of the Chriftian world, no pains were fpared to make
up the breach as foon as poffible. *Dio-
nyfius*, bifhop of *Alexandria*, writing to
Novatian, who had made fome difturbance
in the church of *Rome*, exhorts him to
extinguifh the fchifm; for that it was
better to fuffer any thing, than that the
church of God fhould be rent in pieces[k].
The fchifms of the *Donatifts* and *Novatians* are very ftriking inftances of the
fenfe of the church in general of fuch
matters in thofe days. And how feverely
they branded all fchifm and divifion, and
how induftrioufly they laboured to reconcile diffenting brethren, might eafily be
fhewn from the writers of thofe times[l].

Each particular church had authority
over its own members; and all who lived

[1] Cypr. *De Unitate Ecclefia.*
[k] Eufeb. *Eccl. Hift. lib.* vi. *cap.* 45.
[l] See Cave's *Prim. Chrift.* p. 417.

within

within the pale of it were subject to its
jurisdiction; to the rule of faith, and mode
of worship which it prescribed; and to the
rites and ceremonies ordained by it: And,
when doubts and differences arose, its authority in explaining doctrines, and de-
ciding controversies, was generally acknowledged, resorted to, and acquiesced in.

When false doctrines had crept into one
church, it was thought necessary for other
churches, which had not been infected by
them, to remonstrate against them, and
to declare and assert their own principles:
And, when corruptions in principle, doctrine, and practice, became general in the
church of *Rome*, and had rendered the
terms of its communion sinful, and therefore necessary to be departed from, which
otherwise would have been unjustifiable;
confessions of faith were set forth, in all
the reformed churches, to declare the purity of their doctrines, in opposition to the
errors and corruptions of that church.

This was thought necessary to be done,
among the rest, by the church of *England*;

land; and her authority for this purpose, though now called in queftion, was juftified by the practice of all other churches; and was in itfelf abfolutely indifpenfable, in order to teftify to the world what fhe profeffed, and what fhe reformed from ; as well as to maintain her own confiftency, and *unity in the faith.*

This is what I come in the next place to fpeak to.

How early and careful a regard was paid to this great principle of unity at the *Reformation,* appears from the proceedings of the *Reformers* in that great work; who carried it on with all the prudence, expedition, and attention, that a matter of fuch importance required, and the temper of the times would admit of. In the year 1548, the fecond of King *Edward's* reign, a new *liturgy* was compiled ; and the uniform ufe of it was enjoined by act of parliament ; and enforced from time to time by fubfequent acts of parliament, in that reign, and in the reigns of Queen *Elizabeth,* and *Charles* II. In the year 1552,

the

the main doctrine of the church was set forth, in the articles of religion, which were *agreed upon by the bishops, and other learned men*, for the professed purpose *of avoiding diversities of opinions, and establishing consent concerning true religion.* Those articles were revised, and without any material alterations, were unanimously *agreed upon, by the Arch-bishops and Bishops of both provinces, and the whole Clergy in convocation, in the year* 1562, *for avoiding*, as before, *diversities of opinion, and stablishing consent touching true religion.* And they were *put forth by the Queen's authority.*

Among other points of faith settled by these articles, they authorized the two books of *Homilies*, which contained *a godly and wholesome doctrine necessary for those times*; and which the clergy were required to use for the instruction of the people; whereby both the one, and the other, had found principles instilled into their minds, and were kept steady in them; and these were very seasonable antidotes and preservatives

vatives againſt the falſe doctrines of the church of *Rome* on the one hand; and againſt the wild notions of the enthuſiaſts of thoſe times on the other.

And thus wiſe proviſion was made for uniformity of worſhip, and unity of doctrine, in this church, at its firſt eſtabliſhment; in which it hath continued ever ſince. Its government and diſcipline was then ſettled likewiſe upon the ſame plan, on which it ſtands at preſent: And, upon the whole, our *Jeruſalem is built as a city, that is at unity in itſelf*[m]. She doth not boaſt of perfection, any more than other human conſtitutions. *Nevertheleſs, as far as ſhe hath already attained, ſhe walketh by the ſame rule,* according to the apoſtle's advice[n]. She hath been ever ſteady in her principles; but not ſo rigid and bigoted, as to pay no attention to improvement: For all unprejudiced perſons muſt allow, that her late divines have actually improved upon thoſe who went before them,

---

[m] Pſ. cxxii. 3.   [n] Phil. iii. 16.

in

in their explanations of fome of her doctrines; which being of a more abftrufe
and fpeculative nature; and being judged
by many to be of lefs importance, and to
be fuch as may be held either way, without detriment to the true faith; if our divines of later times have underftood thofe
doctrines with more latitude, and have put
a more liberal conftruction upon them,
than they had before been generally underftood in; and if all are allowed to abound
in their own fenfe of thofe doctrines; this
wrong, if it can be fo called, may furely
be forgiven them. The doctrines I mean,
are thofe chiefly which relate to *predefti-
nation and grace.* It is well known, and
hath been often proved to the fatisfaction
of all unprejudiced perfons, that the
church never meant in her articles, or
elfewhere, to lay down any reftrictive de-
finition of thofe doctrines; but was more
wifely planned upon fuch catholick and
comprehenfive principles, as the moft moderate of all denominations might embrace; fteering a middle courfe between
the

the *Lutherans* and *Calvinists* on the one
hand, and between the *Calvinists* and the
Arminians on the other; but never for-
mally, or expresly, lifting under the
banner of, or attaching herself to, either
party. Her doctrines were settled before
any of her divines went to *Geneva,* or
elsewhere abroad. When they returned,
she had no reason either to condemn, or
espouse, the doctrines they preached; nor
those of *Arminius,* who appeared afterwards. Whatever differences arose with
regard to those doctrines, the church of
England never fell into divisions, nor ba-
nished from her communion, much less
persecuted, any on account of them; as
some foreign protestant churches have
done; and as we daily see is done among
some of our sectaries at home.

On the contrary, though the zeal of the
old *Puritans* for the doctrines of *Calvin*
carried them to such lengths, that they
branded the moderate opinions of those,
who differed from them, as popish, or
tending to popery; yet those opinions
grew

grew by degrees to be the general doctrines of our Englifh divines; and that without noife or difturbance; and I hope too, without having given any caufe to fufpect, they have fince been, or at this time are, more popifhly inclined than formerly.

No imputation of popery can lie againft thofe who hold thefe doctrines either way; becaufe, if there are fome in the church of *Rome*, who underftand them in the moderate fenfe, there are others in that church, the *Molinifts* I mean, who maintain the moft rigid fenfe of them; and thofe Proteftants, who agree with them in this refpect, would not therefore be thought to verge towards popery. Proteftants in general agree with papifts in doctrines more fundamental than thefe.

I believe the *Methodifts* alone, in whom the old *Puritans* feem to be revived, make the rigid fenfe of thefe doctrines, to be, in a manner, the fole teft of the church of *England*, and even of Chriftianity too. Whence they allow falvation to none but thofe of their own perfuafion.

I   Loud

Loud invectives have been made by others againſt our church, on account of the dark, uncertain manner, in which it leaves theſe doctrines. This the more candid would interpret into a latitude, as it was intended, wiſely calculated to com- prehend perſons who differed in their judgements concerning theſe abſtruſe points, which confeſſedly do not affect the eſſence, or well-being, of Chriſtia- nity; while its fundamental doctrines are ſo clearly and explicitly laid down, as not to admit of any uncertainty.

There is yet another charge, which ſtrikes at the very vitals of the church of *England*, and which it is proper here to take notice of. It hath been confidently aſſerted, " That the church of *England*, " properly ſo called, is not now exiſt- " ing°." And, if ſo, there is an end, not only of its unity, but of its very Being. But, God be praiſed! this is no more than an aſſertion, though ſo bold a

---

° See *Confeſſional*, p. 244. 3d edit.

one,

one, that it might as well be faid, the fun doth not fhine at noon-day. The church of *England* not only exifts, but flourifhes likewife, in fpite of all the efforts of its enemies, outward and inward, to deftroy it: And, we truft, *the gates of hell will never prevail againft it.*

If the author of this affertion knows thofe who profefs themfelves of the church of *England*, but who have departed from her doctrines, and have efpoufed tenets diametrically oppofite to them; he doth not furely mean to call this the fenfe of the church of *England*; nor to denominate this church from fuch apoftate members of it.

I proceed, *Thirdly*, to obferve, that not only all the other proteftant churches, and divines, at and after the Reformation; but even the old Non-conformifts here in *England*, had a deep fenfe of the importance of unity; ftrongly remonftrated againft fchifm, and condemned it, as a great fin, and heinous tranfgreffion.

D   We

We have feen what the fenfe of the primitive church was in this refpect. If we come down to later times, we fhall find, that the moft eminent and learned foreign divines, fince the Reformation, who can leaft be fufpected of partiality to this church, were of the fame fentiments.

No one will object to *Calvin's* teftimony, which is very remarkable to this purpofe. " God," fays he, " fets fuch a value upon " the communion of his church, that he " looks upon him, as an apoftate from his " religion, who wilfully feparates from, " and breaks the unity of, any chriftian " fociety, which hath the true miniftry " of the word and facraments." And farther he faith, " that feparation from " fuch a church is a denial of God and " Chrift ; a deftruction of his truth ; " and a facrilegious and perfidious breach " of the marriage between Chrift and his " fpoufe ᴾ." And he enlarges on the fubject.

With regard to the church of *England* ; *Beza,* and *Bullinger,* and all the learned in

ᴾ Inftit. lib. iv. cap. i. fect. 10.

Europe,

Europe, condemned the feparation from it; and its communion was owned by all the proteftant, and reformed churches abroad. The firft *Puritans* at home, fome of whom were fierce and contentious enough, did not yet chufe to leave the church : But *Sampfon,* and *Humphreys,* and *Fox,* and fe- veral others of the moft learned and re- fpectable among them, lived and died in its communion; and were fuffered to preach, and to enjoy their preferments, to the number of *five hundred,* though they did not conform to it q. Even *Cartwright* himfelf declared on his death-bed, " That " he ferioufly lamented the unneceffary " troubles he had caufed in the church, by " the fchifm he had been the great fomenter " of: And wifhed he was to begin his life " again, that he might teftify to the " world the diflike he had to his former " ways r."

q Bifhop *Maddox's* Anfwer to *Neale,* p. 140. *et feqq.*
r *Strype's* Life of Archbifhop *Whitgift,* book iv. ch. 28.

The

The firſt form of diſcipline, that was ſet up by the *Non-conformiſts*, imported, that it was conſiſtent with the peace of the church [*]. And many miniſters, who ſcrupled ſubſcription, declared that its doctrine, and diſcipline, and worſhip, were ſound, godly, and edifying ; and contained nothing in them to juſtify ſeparation, and make a breach in the unity of the church: Nor were there any, who remonſtrated more ſtrongly, or in ſeverer terms, againſt the ſin and miſchief of the ſchiſm that was then made, than ſome of the *Nonconformiſts* themſelves. Though they feared to ſubſcribe, yet they would not ſeparate ; and they even wrote againſt thoſe of the ſeparation, and that with ſuch zeal, that Mr. *Hilderſham*, a celebrated writer among them, was called, *The maul of the Browniſts* [*]. It may be too galling, to repeat the expreſſions of many of them. It is ſufficient to obſerve in general, that in

* *Fuller's* Ch. Hiſt. book ix. p. 140.
* Archbiſhop *Tenniſon's* Argument for Union, in London Caſes, p. 474.

the

the graveſt, and beſt-tempered confutation of the *Separatiſts,* which was made in the name of the *Non-conformiſts,* it is ſaid, that they incurred the moſt ſhameful and odious reproach of manifeſt ſchiſm. And farther, ſay they, " We hold them all to " be in a dangerous ſtate ; we are loath to " ſay in a damnable ſtate, as long as they " continue in this ſchiſm ʷ."

Even the *Separatiſts* themſelves allowed the doctrine of our church to be ſound; and that ſeparation from it was not juſtifiable for all the blemiſhes, imperfections, and corruptions, which they alledged it laboured under.

The *Non-conformiſts,* on the other hand, maintained, that nothing could juſtify ſeparation from the church, but ſuch corruptions as overthrew the being, or conſtitution of it : And that granting there were many and great corruptions in it, they were not ſuch as did overthrow its conſtitution : And they made uſe of ſeveral

* Biſhop *Stillingfleet's* Unreaſonableneſs of Separation, p. 30.

D 3   arguments

arguments to prove, that the church of *England* was a true church of Chrift; and fuch a one, as from which, whofoever wittingly, and continually feparateth himfelf, cutteth himfelf off from Chrift [w].

. In the difputes between the *prefbyterian* divines and the *Independents*, they mutually charged each other with fchifm; into which the *affembly of divines* refolved the departure of the diffenting brethren from their rule of church-government; and their fetting up of feparate congregations: The *Independents*, on the contrary, alledging, that the great caufe of fchifm had been that ftrict obligation of all to uniformity; which the *affembly of divines* had enjoined; and which they complained was exercifing tyranny over men's confciences [x]. And yet at a meeting of diffenting preachers, held in the year 1663, about the lawfulnefs of communicating with the church of *England*, one of them

---

[w] *Stillingfleet*, ib. p. 36.
[x] *Stillingfleet's* Sermon on *Phil.* iii. 16. p. 34.

relatos,

relates, that he had brought in *twenty* reafons, to prove the lawfulnefs of it: And
no one of the brethren, as he adds, feemed
to diffent, but to take the reafons to be
valid[y].

But farther: Such was the fenfe that
the refpective parties, who engaged in *the
folemn league and covenant,* had of the importance of unity in the church, that the
chief defign of it was to unite the three
kingdoms of *England, Scotland,* and *Ireland,* in doctrine, worfhip, difcipline, and
government. Accordingly they ftipulated,
that they would endeavour to bring the
churches of God in the three kingdoms
to the neareft conjunction and uniformity
in religion; confeffing of faith; form of
church-government; and directory for
worfhip and catechifing—that they might
live in faith and love—remain conjoined
in a firm peace and union to all pofterity—
and not fuffer themfelves to be divided, or
withdrawn from, this bleffed union and
conjunction——but conftantly continue

[y] *Ib.* p. 21.

D 4 therein

therein againſt all oppoſition; and promote
the ſame againſt all lets and impediments
whatſoever. And the obſervation of this
league and covenant they engaged to en-
force by all the means in their power.
And they were moſt certainly right in
the general principle, which they went
upon.

Mr. *Hales* is well known to have treated
ſchiſm as lightly as moſt men; and his
tract on that ſubject was eagerly caught
up, as ſoon as it appeared; and much ſtreſs
hath been laid upon his authority ever
ſince: And yet in that very tract he ſaith,
" That communion is the very ſtrength
" and ground of all ſociety; and ſchiſm is
" eccleſiaſtical ſedition—and that to break
" the knot of union is a crime hardly
" pardonable." No enemy to the authors
of ſchiſm can place this ſin in a worſe
light, than their friends have done.

Biſhop *Burnet's* moderation, as a divine,
is acknowledged by all; and yet he treats
ſchiſm as a very grievous ſin. He reckons
it, both in its nature and conſequences, to
be

be one of the greateſt of ſins ; which diſ-
ſolves chriſtian union ; diſlocates the members of Chriſt's body ; creates needleſs di-
ſturbances in the church ; gives occaſion
to all that alienation of mind, all thoſe
raſh cenſures, and unjuſt judgements,
which do ariſe from ſuch diviſions ; which
gives ſcandal to the weak ; and which nothing can juſtify, but the impoſing of un-
lawful terms of communion [z]. But this,
if it ever hath been laid to the charge of the
church of *England,* yet never hath been,
nor ever can be, proved againſt it. The
old diſſenters were ready to ſubſcribe all
our doctrinal articles, and profeſſed greater
zeal for many of them, than they allowed
ſome of our own divines did. Alas! how
are theſe people fallen from their firſt
love! Were any of their fore-fathers now
living, with what vehemence and indig-
nation would they upbraid their ſons for
their degeneracy, in refuſing to ſubſcribe

[z] Biſhop *Burnet* on Article XXXIV. Of the ſin-
fulneſs and miſchief of ſchiſm more at large, ſee
Dodwell on ſchiſm.

any

any of them? They themſelves acknow-
lodge, that their religious ſentiments are
greatly changed from what they were formerly. I wiſh they could ſay, they are
changed for the better. All true ſons of
the church of *England* muſt conclude,
that the change is for the worſe: And God
forbid, that ſuch corruptions in the fundamental doctrines of Chriſtianity, and ſuch
defections from the faith, as are ſo notorious among us, ſhould be countenanced
by law; the ſanction of which was never
obtained for principles of this kind in any
chriſtian country: Much leſs I hope will
it be granted, in any degree, to principles
ſo different from, I might ſay, ſo oppoſite
to, thoſe of the church by law eſtabliſhed.

Our church ſtill perſeveres in the ſame
plan of unity in ſound doctrine, and uniformity of pure worſhip, as ſhe was at firſt
eſtabliſhed upon; agreeably to the nature
and genius of the goſpel.

By purſuing this plan, ſhe not only endeavours to preſerve her own members from
diſſolving the bond of this union; but ſhe
                                    farther

fárthe̊r extends her care to thofe that have feparated from her; in order to prevent that feparation from becoming total. They at prefent profefs to agree with her in doc-trine; and fhe wifhes to preferve that ágreement, being loath to part with them éntirely. It is true, the ligament is but flender: But, while it lafts, it is poffible it may gain ftrength in time. But, if it be cut off, we may then bid farewel to all hopes of a reconciliation. And, if that prove to be the cafe, the guilt will not fall upon' her. Let them look to it, who force themfelves from her embraces. If fhe were to confult her own feparate intereft only, fhe would connive at—fhe would encourage the Diffenters petition for ex-emption from fubfcribing her articles: And, if they underftood the intereft of their own body, they would not defire it; as every fect of them would·dwindle, and fall into decay, the fafter for it.

This they may be affured of, from the experience of former ages, and from the obfervation of thófe, whofe opinions they can have no objection to. It was the remark of *Socrates*, the ecclefiaftical hiftorian, on occafion of the fchifms of the *Arians*, *Novatians*, and others; that, when a breach is once made in the church, it feldom refts there: But thofe who made it begin a frefh quarrel with each other, and upon very flight pretences become divided among themfelves[a].

This hath been confirmed in all ages; and they may fee abundant proofs of it in the prefent. It was then confirmed in fact, when the *Novatians*, and *Donatifts*, fubdivided themfelves; and cut themfelves, as well as the whole church, *minutatim*, and *fruftum de frufto*, as St. *Auftin* complains[b]. For a judicious hiftorian obferves, "That as the *Novatians* feparated "from the antient orthodox church; fo "did the fect of the *Quarto-decimani*, from

---

[a] 'Η γαρ εκκλησια διαιρεθεισα, επι τη απαξ γινομενη διαιρεσει ουχ ισαlο· αλλα σραφενlες καθ' εαυlων παλιν εχωρυν' και μικρας, και ευlελους προφασεως λαβομενοι, αλληλων διεχωριζοnlo. Socr. Hift. Ecclef. lib. v. c. 20. Vide etiam c. 21. 23, 24.

[b] Per tot divifiones feipfos minutatim — conciderunt. *Aug.* contra *Parm.* lib. ii. cap. 18. Præcidens de frufto fruftum, et non fe dolens ab integritate præcifum. *Aug.* enarr. in Pf. xxxvi. 2.

the

" the *Novatians;* And the *Donatifts* were
" fubdivided into the *Rogatifts, Maximini-*
" *anifts, Parmenianifts, Cirrenfes, Circum-*
" *celliones,* and many other fects. And the
" fame thing," fays he, " have we feen
" to happen in our own time. The *Lu-*
" *therans,* after having feparated from the
" reft of the proteftant churches, were
" immediately fplit into *Flaccians, Ofian-*
" *drians,* and the like. We fee," as he
farther obferves, " the Englifh *Puritans*
" are feparating from the church, and
" from one another every day. But, above
" all, the *Anabaptifts* are remarkable on
" this account; who have fo many fects
" fwarming among them, that fcarce any
" can reckon their number, or names°."

When the church of *England* had been
fuppreffed by the parliament; and the prefbyterian difcipline, fo highly applauded,
and fo long and earneftly contended for,
was fet up in its ftead; it likewife, in its
turn, foon experienced diffenters from itfelf, as the church of *England* had done

° *Brandt's* Hiftory of the Reformation, vol. II.
book xxiv. p. 228.

D 7   before;

before: Who though at firft but inconfiderable in number, yet in a few years
grew, and multiplied fo faft, ftill dividing
as they increafed, that " they brake into
" fractions of fractions ;" and fuch fwarms
of fectaries of all forts appeared, as were
never known in this nation, either before,
or fince. " Infomuch that the minifters
" of the province of *London* expreffed the
" ftate of things, in the year 1647, in this
" manner: *Inftead of unity and uniformity*
" *in matters of religion, we are torn in pieces*
" *with diftractions, fchifms, feparations, di-*
" *vifions, and fubdivifions* [d]."

The firft fruits of the toleration, which
appeared among the diffenters, were their
quarrels and difputes with each other, on
points of fmall importance [e].

The *Methodifts*, we all know, had fcarce
appeared, before they began to be divided
under their refpective leaders; and they
continue to be more and more divided
ftill. And the *Independents* fet up on the
principle of divifion, diametrically oppofite

[d] See archbifhop *Tenifon's* Argument for Union, in
London Cafes, p. 462.

[e] See *Calamy's* Life of *Baxter, Anno* 1689, *et feqq.*

to

to that of the gofpel. For, in the congre-
gational way, every congregation is a com-
plete and feparate church ; and there may
be as many religions as churches. But as
they, and the diffenters in general, are better
acquainted with their own hiftory, and
conftitutions, than I am able to inform
them ; I need only appeal to themfelves for
the truth of what is here advanced, and the
confequences of it. They themfelves feel,
and complain, that their intereft, upon the
whole, is on the decline ; which cannot
more juftly be attributed to any one caufe,
nor to any one more natural, than to their
own differences.

The weaknefs of the *independent* government, and its infufficiency to fupport itfelf,
was experienced in *New-England*, as by
others, fo particularly by Mr. *Roger Willi-
ams* ; who went on refining, and proceeded
in his feparation from the church of *Salem*,
of which he had been preacher, fo far, as at
laft to diffolve his fociety ; declaring, that
every one fhould have liberty to worfhip
God according to the light of his own confcience *.

* *Stillingfleet*, Unreafonab. of Separation, p. 113. 293.

That

That this kind of church government subsists at all, much less flourishes, there, or elsewhere, cannot be owing to its own constitution, *as such*; which is so ill calculated for that of a national church [f].

No

[f] This suggests the following remarks on the state of the church of *England*, in *America*.

First, It is well known, that the church of *England* in that country hath many difficulties to struggle with: Notwithstanding it is observable, that, like the primitive church, she thrives under her pressures, having been generally gaining ground there, among all the other denominations of Christians, with which she is intermixt. A most manifest proof of the superior excellence of her constitution!

But, Secondly, Her present situation is very critical, as her clergy have for some time been under a state of persecution in some of the colonies, who have thought fit to revenge their quarrels with the mother-country upon them; which shews what spirit they are of. This renders the case of the former truly deplorable; but yet, we trust, not quite desperate. For,

Thirdly, As the Divine Providence often brings good out of evil, they will have a comfortable prospect of deliverance, by the interposition of government; when it is to be hoped the present disturbances will end in peace; and the respective rights of the mother-country, and her colonies, will be thoroughly settled. And all other grievances being removed, we may humbly hope likewise, that the distressed church of *England* will not be overlooked: But that she will be placed

upon

. No one remonſtrated more, nor more ſtrongly, nor indeed wrote better, againſt the great miſchief of diviſions and ſeparations, than Mr. *Richard Baxter*; the fatal effects of which he foretels in theſe words. " Separation," ſays he, " will ruin the ſe-" parated churches themſelves at laſt. It " will admit of no conſiſtency. Parties " will ariſe in the ſeparated churches, and " ſeparate again from them, till they are

upon an equal footing with all other proteſtant churches; and be allowed the common privilege, which none other is deprived of, the ordaining of her own miniſters. For which purpoſe it is neceſſary ſhe ſhould have an eſtabliſhment of biſhops, inveſted with proper authority over their own clergy; which is all that is deſired; and without any ſecular power whatſoever. This grant, ſo juſt and reaſonable in itſelf, and which hath ſo long been ſolicited for, would at this time be a ſeaſonable relief and recompence to the poor clergy, for their ſufferings in the cauſe of government: Who, as by principle they are, and, in theſe trying times, have approved themſelves to be, well affected to our go-, vernment, in the ſtate, as well as the church; this would give them more conſequence, and better enable them to preſerve peace, and promote loyalty in, the colonies hereafter. The hands of government would likewiſe be ſtrengthened, by their mutual ſupport, and by the conſequent increaſe of ſo conſiderable a body of their beſt friends.

E

" diſ-

" diffolved ⁵." " Men may chufe one paftor
" to-day, and another to-morrow, and fo
" turn round, till they are giddy, and run
" themfelves out of breath—till they
" fit down, and reft in irreligion and
" atheifm ʰ." Would God, this obfervation were not too truly verified in our
days !

In this view, it is a queftion, Whether
the toleration, in effect, hath proved of
all that benefit to the diffenters, which
was expected ; as probably it was a means
of weakening the diffenting intereft, which
feems to have been rather on the decline
ever fince: And therefore, if it were extended farther, I do not apprehend this
indulgence would be detrimental to the
church, any otherwife, than as it would hurt
religion in general, among all forts and denominations of chriftians ; and bring on a
greater relaxation of religious principle,
which is growing upon us too faft already.
Divifion, it is true, weakens the main
body ; but, as long as the feveral parts are

ᵍ Unreafonablenefs of Separation, *ib.* p. 113,
ʰ *Ib.* p. 203.

divided

divided from each other, they weaken themfelves more: And our common Chriftianity fuffers between them.

But the church of *England* hath found out the fecret of defeating the ill effects of the divifions made from it, in a great meafure. Charity is political wifdom. The moderation of government in church and ftate, and its forbearance in putting the laws in execution, which ftill remain in force againft the diffenters, hath in a manner difarmed them. And there is befides, by a kind difpofition of Providence, a ftrong tendency in every wound made, in the political, as well as natural body, to clofe and heal itfelf; whereby it contributes to repair the damage it hath done.

I have been led into thefe reflections on our divifions, and their confequences, taken in a political view. I cannot quit this fubject without confidering them in their religious nature; and confequences likewife.

Schifm, as we have feen, and as it always hath been underftood, is fo odious in

its nature, and fo invidious in its application,
that the charge and imputation of it hath
of late been laid afide; and the very term itfelf in a manner quite dropt; out of polite-
nefs, I prefume, towards thofe who might
be thought liable to it : And the act of toleration, having given the diffenters a kind
of eftablifhment, may have induced them,
and others to think that charge not to be
now applicable to them : And hence they
have come to think our religious differences, and diverfities of opinion, to have
little or no harm in them ; infomuch that
a very confiderable body of proteftant diffenters, who would be thought to make a
majority of the whole, feem to queftion,
whether there be any evil in them or not.
" If diverfities of opinion be an evil"—
fay they, in the Cafe of proteftant diffenting
minifters, and fchool-mafters, addreffed to
parliament in the year 1773.

I fhould be glad to draw a veil over a
matter of this delicacy, and be extremely
forry to rip up any old fores unneceffarily.
But the fkinning them over too foon,
                                    before

before they are throughly healed, is a falfe
tendernefs, and a flattering of the com-
plaint, inftead of removing it. It is better
to fearch, and probe the wound to the
bottom ; to deal honeftly, though harfhly,
where the cafe requires fuch treatment ;
and to call things by their right names,
though they fhould not be the moft plea-
fant to the ear.

Neither time, nor prefcription, nor
the opinions of men, can alter the nature of things ; nor is an evil, grown
into inveterate habit, to be looked upon
as cured. What was fchifm two hundred
years ago, is fchifm ftill. We have feen
what a grievous fin this is, in the fcripture account ; and in the eftimatiou of all
former ages. No favourable views, in
which of late it hath been reprefented,
can render it in the leaft more innocent
at prefent. The *toleration* can have no
efficacy for the overcoming of its malig-
nancy. Indeed, the very term itfelf fup-
pofes its continuance as a *grievance* at leaft ;
and every grievance, as fuch, is an evil.

E 3 And

And as a *grievance,* it is *tolerated;* fince it neither can, nor ought, confiftently with the laws of the gofpel, any more than with the laws of the land, to be removed.

I do not undertake to charge any of our proteftant diffenting brethren with the formal guilt of this fin: But it becomes them very ferioufly to confider themfelves, how far any of them are chargeable with it. *To their own mafter they ftand, or fall.* This I am confident of, that the church of *England* is very fafe from having given any juft caufe for our divifions. She hath never driven any from her; and the diffenters themfelves have acknowledged the lawfulnefs of her communion, by their conforming occafionally to it. She may therefore wafh her hands from any guilt in this refpect.

Great allowances are undoubtedly to be made for thofe who have been born, and brought up, in other communions, even fuppofing them to be fchifmatical, being fincere and well-meaning Chriftians; as I hope, and believe, they in general are; and
withal

withal *zealous of the traditions of their fa-
thers.* Notwithſtanding, the ſin itſelf is,
in its own nature, ſtill the ſame. But there
are others, of whom we cannot think ſo
favourably. Many, too many, I fear, there
are, who, not content to tread in the foot-
ſteps of their fore-fathers, have *diſſented*
even from them, as well as from the
church; and that in ſome of the moſt eſ-
ſential doctrines of Chriſtianity; which
greatly aggravates the guilt of their ſchiſm.
And there are others ſtill, ſome of whom
are gone out from among ourſelves, *wan-
dering ſtars,* who *deſpiſe dominion, ſpeak evil
of dignities, and ſeparate themſelves;* and
become authors and abettors of new ſects;
as if we were not ſufficiently divided already. Theſe all think themſelves fully
juſtified, by taking ſhelter under the act of
toleration. But that is no protection to
them from the laws of God, though it is
from the law of the land. We can only
leave them, and their followers, to the
mercy of God, and their own reflections;
and to the feelings of their own conſciences;

which

which it is to be hoped will difpofe them to think more foberly of themfelves, and to return to Chrift's flock, from which they have ftrayed.

As it hath been fhewn, that the firft care of the church of *England* was to eftablifh unity of doctrine, and uniformity of worfhip in itfelf, fo effential to its conftitution; I come now,

Fourthly, To confider the right, wifdom, and utility, of requiring fubfcription to its articles of faith and religion, in order to this end.

It hath been already obferved, that it was the practice of all the reformed churches, at their firft eftablifhment, to draw up and fettle fome certain confeffions of faith, as the ftandard of the doctrines they profeffed, in oppofition to the errors of the church of *Rome*; and as a teftimony to the world of the foundnefs of their own principles; which they required their own members, either explicitly, or tacitly, to give their affent to; and which they likewife folicited, and

generally

generally obtained, from other reformed churches.

And from this general practice, the church of *England* was countenanced, and sufficiently justified, in doing the same. Nay, this put her under an unavoidable necessity of conforming to all the other churches of the Reformation in this respect. For, had she omitted to follow their example, it would not be known how far she meant to carry the Reformation. Her own members would not have known, what particular doctrines she maintained; nor what erroneous opinions, or corrupt practices, she rejected, and protested against. And, had she shewn any backwardness in this respect, there would have been just cause to suspect her inclination to reform at all—that she halted between two opinions, and had still a secret hankering after the church of *Rome.*

That some provision of this kind was useful and wise, at the critical juncture in which it was made; in order to restore

the

the faith to its original purity, and to purge it from the defilements which it had contracted ; and was expedient, and even neceſſary to be continued, in the trying times which have ſucceeded, to preſerve it in the ſame pure and found ſtate which it had been reſtored to ; any thinking perſon will ſoon be convinced, who conſiders, the importance of the Reformation ; the difficulties which the firſt reformers had to encounter; and the dangers with which this church hath ever ſince been ſurrounded : And it is owing to the diſtance of time ; and thoſe difficulties having been ſurmounted; and to the dangers being not ſo apparent; that many in theſe days do not apprehend the neceſſity of continuing the meaſures that have been taken; which, if they were to enter more deeply into them, they would find to be perhaps no leſs uſeful and neceſſary ſtill ; if not more ſo, from new dangers and difficulties, ariſing from the quarters of infidelity, as well as from popery itſelf. The more, and the greater our dangers are ; the more,

in

in common prudence, we fhould be upon
our guard ; and the more collected in ourfelves, to withftand them. The more
dangerous and numerous the enemies of
the crofs of Chrift are; the more we
fhould hold faft the profeffion of our
faith ; and the more we fhould be united
in it.

It hath been already obferved, that the
chief provifion which our church hath
made, for preferving an unity of faith and
doctrine, is that of the *Thirty-nine articles of religion*; the profeffed defign of
which is, as before obferved from the import of their title, *for the avoiding of diverfities of opinion, and for the ftablifhing of
confent concerning true religion.* And they
are of excellent ufe for this purpofe, as in
fact they prove to have been. Even with
refpect to inert matter, the firmnefs of it
confifts in the cohefion of its parts; and
in two material bodies, the more points of
contact in which they meet, the more
they adhere to each other.

Now,

Now, the articles of the church of *Eng-land* may be confidered as fo many points of contact, in which its members unite, and adhere to each other; and the whole body is kept together in its original ftate; and hath, without any confiderable alteration, been preferved in that ftate ever fince the Reformation.

The author of the *Confeffional* owns it to be "a fact, in which our hiftorical writers "of all parties agree, that, during the "reign of Queen *Elizabeth*, and fome part "of the reign of King *James* I. there was "no difference between the epifcopal "churchmen and the *Puritans* in matters "of doctrine[1]." And again, fays he, "The doctrinal articles were fubfcribed "by all parties, without referve; becaufe "the opinions of all parties were tolerably "uniform, with refpect to the fubject "matter of them[2]."

He might have purfued this branch of hiftory farther; and found, that this uniformity was continued till the church

[1] *Confeffional*, p. 270.   [2] *Ib.* p. 281.

itfelf,

itfelf, together with fubfcription to its articles, and all its other ordinances, was
fuppreffed under the Commonwealth; and
the prefbyterian and independent difcipline
was fubftituted in its ftead,—That fubfcription to the articles in general, was revived at the reftoration of the government
in church and ftate—That on the toleration it was enacted by law, that the doctrinal articles were ftill to be fubfcribed—
and that accordingly they have been fubfcribed, or have been fuppofed to be fubfcribed, by all of whom fubfcription is required, to this very day. Whence it appears, there was ftill little or no difference
between the epifcopal churchmen, and the
diffenters in matters of doctrine—and that
the opinions of all parties were all along
tolerably uniform, with refpect to the fub-
ject-matter of the articles. And they
have thus proved an effectual means of
preventing diverfities of opinion, and efta-
blifhing confent concerning true religion:
And that muft be deemed the general confent of this church and nation, as long as
they

they continue to be fubfcribed; whatever may be infinuated, or pleaded to the contrary, from the diverfities of opinion entertained by particular perfons, often in contradiction to their own fubfcriptions; which cannot in juftice be laid to the account of the church. And upon thefe grounds, and in this fenfe, thofe divines might juftly affert this conftant agreement of doctrine, who are ridiculed on this account in the *Confeffional* [1].

As fubfcription to the articles hath been an effectual means of preferving the doctrines of the church in general; fo hath it been particularly ferviceable in keeping the church of *England* free from the falfe doctrines and corruptions of popery.

But, as bifhop *Burnet* obferves, " That " many had complied with every altera- " tion, both in King *Henry's,* and King " *Edward's* reign; who not only declared " themfelves to have been all the while " papifts; but became bloody perfecutors,

[1] P. 153. 156. See *ib.* p. 322. Note.

" in

" in Queen *Mary's* days[m];" the author of
the *Confeſſional* hence infers, " that the re-
" quiring of ſubſcription to articles of re-
" ligion was an ineffectual meaſure for
" excluding all from the miniſtry, who
" had any tincture of popery." And this,
he ſays, " the good biſhop here con-
" feſſes;" though the biſhop ſays no ſuch
thing. And upon theſe grounds he con-
demns Queen *Elizabeth's* biſhops; and all
ſucceeding impoſers of ſubſcription, for
continuing ſuch an ineffectual teſt[n].

But hath it proved ſo ineffectual in fact,
upon the whole, or in any period after the
above-mentioned?

That many ſhould give way to the
times at the beginning of the Reformation, when its principles were not fully
ſettled; and ſhould prevaricate, and com-
ply with every alteration that was made;
and ſhould afterwards throw off the maſk,
when they ſaw the church of *Rome,* in
which they had been bred, and had ſo

[m] Introduction to Expoſition of Articles, p. 4.
[n] Confeſſional, *ib.*

lately

lately left, again become predominant; is not at all to be wondered at. It is not said, that any of thefe were of the clergy, or had fubfcribed to the articles of religion; and fuppofing, as is probable, there were fome of them among thofe falfe brethren, yet it is not fair to make an eftimate of the efficacy of any means, from fuch partial and uncertain proofs, and fuch unfettled times, which did not admit of a fair trial of them. Let this writer carry his enquiries down to the times which fucceeded the eftablifhment of the Reformation under Queen *Elizabeth*; and he will not find *many*, if any, among the clergy of the church of *England*, from thofe times to the prefent, who fubfcribed to the articles of religion, and were afterwards detected to have been papifts; or, as he puts the cafe, even *to have had any tincture of popery* in them.

Some few inftances, I allow there have been in former times, of apoftates among the clergy, from the church of *England* to that of *Rome*; but none that I can
recollect

recollect of difguifed papifts continuing to officiate, or to hold preferments in it; much lefs in any fuch numbers, as to juftify the above-mentioned inference; that fubfcription to the articles is an ineffectual meafure for excluding papifts from the miniftry. If this writer knew of any fuch, I prefume he would not have failed to produce them.

We may therefore appeal to the annals of our church, and to the facts contained in them, which are always the moft decifive proofs; and they will authorize us to conclude, That fubfcription to the articles of religion hath been a moft effectual means of keeping papifts out of the miniftry of our church. For to what other caufe can this be fo juftly afcribed, as to the many *fences* which are raifed againft the fundamental errors and corruptions of popery, in our articles, and in our liturgy? The former are fo cautioufly, fo clearly, and fo ftrongly worded, that papifts, and even *Jefuits*, with all their fophiftry and equivocation, have not been

F able

able to break through, or furmount them. And our excellent liturgy is framed in a manner fo diametrically oppofite to the idolatrous worfhip of the church of *Rome,* that almoft every office and prayer of it would flafh conviction in the face of any prieft of that church, who fhould have the hardinefs to ufe it.

Inftances there have been, in abundance, of popifh priefts and *Jefuits,* appearing under the difguife of *Quakers, Independents,* and other fectaries; becaufe none of thofe fects had any fpecial provifions againft them°. But though the emiffaries of *Rome* have appeared in all fhapes to fo-ment our differences; yet I do not know of their having ever been found to perfo-nate the clergy of the church of *England,*

° *Quakerifm* is faid to have been hatcht at *Rome.* The fect of the *Seekers* hath been traced to the fame origin; and both are fuppofed to have been actuated from thence; popifh factors having been found to mix themfelves in great numbers with thofe, and other fec-taries; preaching in their affemblies; plotting the death of King *Charles* the Firft; and diffeminating the moft infernal politicks among them. For this fee *Ca-lamy's* Life of *Baxter,* vol. I. p. 57—60. 100, 101, 102.

either

either in, or out of it; unlefs it be in one
inftance; and whether that makes more
for, or againft, the purport of what is here
advanced, let the reader judge.

The inftance I mean is that of *Faithful
Cummin*; whofe ftory ought not to pafs
here unnoticed. This man appeared in
the year 1566, under the difguife of a
diffenting preacher. He would exercife ex-
temporary prayer for two hours together;
groaning and weeping, in a congregation
he had gathered of *men of tender confciences*, as he called them. He pretended to the fpirit, and to make the
church purer than it was. He preached
againft fet forms of prayer; called the
Englifh liturgy the *Englifh mafs*; and had
perfuaded feveral to pray fpiritually, and
ex tempore. And, what feemed in a manner
peculiar to him, he, by fome means or
other, would get into the church, and
preach againft *Rome* and the *Pope*; but
took care never to appear till divine fervice
was over; nor to join either in the *Englifh*
liturgy, or in receiving the facrament, in
the church of *England*. Being detected,

he

he proved to be a *Dominican fryar*; and said he had been ordained by *cardinal Pole*. Having fled from *England*, and gone to *Rome*, he was imprifoned by the *Pope*, *Pius* V, for railing at him, and his church, in *England*. But he convinced his Holinefs of his having, under that colour, done him, and mother-church, fo much fervice; by the *odium* which he had caft upon the church of *England*, and the ftumbling-block which he had laid in its way, that the *Pope* rewarded him with a prefent of two thoufand ducats[p].

To proceed. Upon the whole of what hath been faid, I do not fee what objection any good proteftant, or any one, but a downright papift, can poffibly have againft the continuance of fubfcription to the articles againft popery, above all others. For can any renunciation of the church of *Rome*, and of its erroneous and corrupt doctrines, be too explicit, againft the fubtle diftinctions, equivocations, and mental refervations of that church?

[p] *Strype's* Life of Archbifhop *Parker*, book III. ch. xiii. xvi. p. 230. 244.

But,

But, inftead of fubfcription to the articles againft popery, it is propofed, That a declaration fhould be required of perfons, who offer themfelves for orders, or preferment in the church, and for the miniftry out of it, *That they are proteftants.* But what will this one general declaration avail towards keeping papifts out of either? will a *Jefuit* fcruple to declare himfelf a *proteftant?* and if he is called upon to explain himfelf, which no body will have power to compel him to, will it not readily occur to him to fay, That he meant only to *proteft* againft the tyranny of the *pope,* in diffolving his order, and depriving him and his fraternity of their poffeffions?

Our proteftant diffenters always dreaded popery, as their moft deadly enemy; and thought they could fcarce ever be fufficiently fafe from it. And their jealoufy of it carried them fo far, as to tax the church of *England* with being papiftical, or popifhly inclined, for having any thing in common with the church of *Rome*;

F 3   the

the leaft rag of which they could not bear the thoughts of. And are all their appre-henfions, and hatred of it, come to this at laft? Hath popery changed its nature? And is it now fo little formidable, that they can be content with the bare profeffion of their being proteftants; and need nothing more to protect them from it? Is it for fear of offending the delicacy of the Roman catholicks, that they dare not fo much as add, that *they are not papifts?* I hope, when they next apply to parlia-ment, they will think fome ftronger bulwark neceffary to be raifed againft popery. Sure I am, that they cannot give it any greater advantages, than by thus fu-pinely expofing themfelves to the incur-fions of fo watchful an enemy.

Of as little avail, in general, would a declaration, or fubfcription, be, that a perfon was a chriftian; and received the fcriptures as the word of God, and as the rule of his faith and manners. For fub-fcription, in fuch vague and general terms, would be little more than the fhadow of fubfcription,

fubfcription, to fave appearances ; and, at
the fame time, to evade the real intent and
ufe of the law in this refpect. Men may
declare themfelves chriftians, who fcarce
deferve the name, and who hold very anti-
chriftian principles; and it is well known,
that the vileft hereticks have profeffed the
greateft regard for the fcriptures, and have
fheltered themfelves under the umbrage
of them. But to return.

The author of the *Confeffional* is under
great apprehenfions of danger from the
growth of popery among us: And I entirely approve of his zealous endeavours
to excite the vigilance of our governors in
church and ftate againft it, and its emiffaries; and particularly againft the moft
infidious and intriguing of them all, the
Jefuits; who, fince their expulfion from
other kingdoms, muft be fuppofed, and
are known, to difperfe themfelves in great
numbers, in this, and all other proteftant
countries; and to appear in all fhapes,
more than ever. But we do not know
what fecret inftructions they may have to

propagate

propagate popery, and the interest of mother-church; though she seems to have
proved but a step-mother to them.

I agree with him in every thing he says
about our danger from popery, and the
Jesuits particularly; but I can by no
means agree with him, in the inference he
draws from it. " You will ask," says he,
" what has all this to do with subscription
" to articles of religion; and the esta-
" blishment of confessions of faith and
" doctrine, in protestant countries⁹?" We
might know of ourselves, that it certainly
hath something to do with them; but
should never dream of the use he makes
of this; nor ever imagine, that the con-
clusion which he draws from hence is,
That subscription to articles of faith
should—not be enforced, or continued—
but be entirely laid aside—to those very
articles, he must mean, about one half of
which are directly, and in express words,
leveled against the church of *Rome*; which
he is under such dread of. And yet, in the

⁹ See Conf. pref. to first edit. p. c.

same

fame breath, he endeavours to put us out of conceit with thofe articles, among the reft. As well might he go about to per-fuade us, " Neighbours, your lands are " threatened with an inundation ; there-" fore, by all means, down with your em-" bankments; and be fure you level them " all with the ground." " Your houfe is " befet with thieves : Therefore pray " throw open your doors to receive " them." The language of the *Confef-fional, mutatis mutandis,* is, in plain Eng-lifh, none other than this : And he, who talks in this manner, might well be fufpected of being an accomplice, were we not otherwife fully fatisfied of this learned writer's proteftant principles; and it is much to be regretted, that a perfon of fuch abilities fhould be fo far blinded by his bigotry for the caufe he is em-barked in, as to ftudy thus to impofe upon himfelf, and others, by fuch fophiftical reafoning, as will prove *quidlibet ex quo-libet.* But every unprejudiced perfon furely, who hath the free ufe of his fenfes, will

fee,

fee, that the greater our danger is, the more it fhould be guarded againft; and that it is madnefs to throw down barriers and bulwarks, when there is the greateft need of them. I hope therefore our fenators will fuffer the articles, againft popery at leaft, to continue in force, till we have fomething better than a bare declaration, *that we are proteftants,* fubftituted in their ftead.

. Nor would the making, and fubfcribing, the declaration againft popery, required by the act of toleration, much mend the matter, were it more explicit than it is. For, to argue with them on their own principles, Are not thefe human forms? are not the very terms unfcriptural? For I believe they will not find the words, *popery, papift,* or *proteftant,* in their bibles. How then can they fubfcribe any fuch confeffions, or declarations, which are not expreffed in the words of fcripture, any more than the *articles* of the church of *England?*

They

. They fcruple fubfcribing thofe, or any other human forms : And yet they can make, and fubfcribe the delaration againſt popery of the 30th Car. II. ſtat. 2. c. 1. which is expreſſed in the hard unfcrip-tural words—*tranfubſtantiation, maſs, pope, equivocation, mental refervation,* &c. What inconfiſtency!

Hence furely we muſt be fully con-vinced of the abfolute neceſſity of fome *human forms*; which it is better to fubmit to, than to condemn them all in the lump; and let men loofe, to run wild after their own vagaries; and to expofe the fimple and unwary to become a prey to the crafty feducer.

Another means which I mentioned, of keeping this church ſtedfaſt in the unity of faith, is, that uniformity of publick worſhip, which is eſtabliſhed by law in it : Whence the reading of the fcriptures of both Old and New Teſtament, more, and more orderly, than I believe in any other church—the frequent repetition of its creeds —the conſtant ufe of the facraments— and

and the interweaving of the fame doctrines in its prayers and offices, which are
contained in the articles—all this corro-
borates, and perpetuates the belief and
profeffion of them; habituates the people
to them, and fixes them in their minds.

Add to this, That the difcourfes of the
clergy from the pulpit, and their printed
works, being generally conformable to
the doctrine of the church, do conftantly
contribute to inculcate and confirm the
truth of it; and to preferve the faith pure
and uncorrupt, and the people ftedfaft in
it, without being *toffed about with every
wind of doctrine.*

If the *fame round of offices* be difguftful
to fome nice palates, there is room to
fufpect their want of a true relifh for devotion; there being fuch a pleafing variety, and alternation, in the feveral parts
of the publick worfhip, according to the
liturgy of the church of *England,* as fufficiently recommends it to all fober and
pious chriftians. It engages, and at the
fame time relieves, our attention; and the
whole

whole is admirably contrived to keep up the fpirit of devotion alive in our fouls, throughout the whole fervice: And if the unftable, and fickle-minded, grow tired of fuch *hackneyed forms*[r]; they muft have more virtue than piety, or at leaft a great happinefs of temper in other refpects, not to be tired of themfelves, and all about them. If fuch perfons had the new-modeling of our liturgy, I wonder how they would contrive it, to make it ever new, and ever pleafing; unlefs they think, that *extempore* effufions would better anfwer that intention; which can come but with an ill grace from any churchman. For our parts, it may not be amifs to liften to the wife man's advice, *not to meddle with them that are given to change.*

We cannot juftly fay, how well calculated the conftitution of other churches, and congregations, among us are, for preferving the chriftian faith found and uncorrupt in them; becaufe they are more

---

[r] See *Confeffional*, p. 18.

referved;

referved ; at leaft, their liturgies, or di-
rectories, are not made fo publick. But,
if we may judge of the tree by its fruit,
the writings of their chief divines appear
in a very different ftrain from, nay are
contrary to, the works of thofe that went
before them ; not only in the doctrines
relating to the divine decrees ; but in the
more important points of the fatisfaction
and divinity of the Son of God ; not to
mention other inftances.

Some confiderable helps, to keep them
ftedfaft and united in the true faith, I apprehend, are wanting in moft, if not all,
our diffenting congregations ; fuch as fome
certain ftandard of doctrine—the ufe of
fome, or other, of the primitive creeds;
and, if I have been rightly informed, none
of them are ufed in the kirk of *Scotland*—
the want of fome fettled forms of prayer
in moft of them—no obfervance of the
great feftivals, and of courfe no fpecial
commemoration of the great mercies of
them. Add to this, that the neglect of
fubfcribing the doctrinal articles, with

5   the

the connivance at it, creates indifference, and makes room for a change of principles.

With regard to difcipline, the old *Puritans* were remarkably ftrict and rigid; but the prefent diffenters in general are fallen into the contrary extreme. The platform fet forth by the former was very narrow, and confined. The latter obferve fuch a latitude, that they fcarce know how to contrive it wide enough '.

Our articles were not Calviniftical enough for the *Geneva* difcipline; and our divines were cenfured for leaning too much to *Arminianifm*. The articles, with

* See *Prieftley's* form of difcipline, in his addrefs to proteftant diffenters. There cannot be a more remarkable inftance of the great relaxation of difcipline among the diffenters, than is to be feen in the perfon of this writer himfelf; who goes on uttering blafphemies, without controul, or rebuke, from his brethren, or indeed from any others; while *Emlyn* was perfecuted in *Ireland*, and *Pierce, Withers*, and *Hallet*, in *England*, by the diffenting clergy; and that within the memory of many now living, for writings much lefs offenfive to all ferious chriftians.

many

many now, are quite too *Calviniftical*; and they have far outgone *Arminius* himfelf. The *Arminian* fenfe of the articles was conftrued formerly, as having a tendency to popery, if not to be papiftical, in arch-bifhop *Laud*, and others, who efpoufed that fenfe. It is now extended much far-ther by thofe who profefs the greateft averfion to popery that can poffibly be ex-preffed [t].

But the main charge of all is, That the requifition of fubfcription to articles of faith in general is fuch an unwarrantable impofition, as is not to be juftified, from any confiderations of ufe, or neceffity; nor from the examples of other churches; being a manifeft infringement on the right of private judgement; the facred and in-violable privilege of all proteftants.

This is a weighty objection, and de-ferves to be very ferioufly confidered: In order to which, it will be requifite to go to the bottom of it; and carefully to exa-mine this right of private judgement, on which it is founded.

[t] See p. 30. *fuprà*.

To

To think, and judge for himſelf, in all matters pertaining to one's ſelf, is what every thinking being hath undoubtedly a very good right to. It is his birth-right, and is inherent in his very nature; nor can he be deprived of it, any more than he can be diveſted of himſelf. Think he muſt; and, as ſelf is ever uppermoſt in his thoughts, he will at all events think for himſelf; and it concerns, and is incumbent upon him, to extend his thoughts to every thing relating to his own welfare, temporal and ſpiritual. And his thoughts are his own, which no man can invade, or diſpoſſefs him of; however he may be reſtrained in the outward workings of them.

On this right the Reformation was founded, nor can it ever be controverted upon proteſtant principles; and God forbid we ſhould ever be deprived of ſo valuable a privilege! But the queſtion is, whether this, in common with all our other rights, natural as well as civil, *in ſociety,* is not liable to ſome reſtraints and

limi-

limitations, in the ufe and refult of it? And whether it hath not its proper fphere of action, within which it ought to be confined?

If we are to take our meafures in this enquiry, from the extent to which this right hath been carried of late, and af-ferted by its modern advocates; we muft conclude, that the right of private judge-ment is abfolute, uncontroulable, and un-alienable [u]. For, from being obliged to have recourfe to this right, on neceffary and juft occafions ; and from a modeft and wary ufe of it, in reforming from the church of *Rome*; men have been em-boldened by degrees to carry it to fuch an extravagant height in all cafes, as to fet it above all controul; and every abridge-ment of it, though made by lawful au-thority, they look upon as an ufurpation. But, if we examine this queftion by the fober rules of reafon and religion, we fhall be convinced, that this, as well as all other rights of men in fociety, muft be

[u] See *Confeffional,* 1ft. edit. p. 194.

I   fubject subject to some limitations, and become subordinate to the superior rights of the society in general.

The right of private judgement, by the very term of its being *private*, must be limited by a man's own private capacity, as an individual; and by the sphere of his own private concerns, in matters which do not affect the publick. This is the proper sphere of its action, as contradistinguished from that of the publick: Nor do men, as highly as they affect to think of it, always give it full scope, even within these bounds; though the same men, in other cases, will not brook the prescribing of any bounds to it.

We are often at a loss in judging for ourselves, not only in spiritual, but in temporal matters likewise, of daily occurrence. In such cases, which come home to us, we perceive the weakness of our own judgements; and, very prudently distrusting them, we think it adviseable to consult our neighbours and friends; and to submit our own to their better

judge-

judgements. In common interefts, common confultations become requifite of courfe. When two, or three, are united in intereft, it is natural for them to unite in council. Their united deliberations they find ftrengthen their judgements, and are productive of riper determinations: And it is not uncommon for them to devolve the management of their whole concerns upon one of their number; in whofe fuperior wifdom and difcretion their experience hath taught them to confide. As the force of their judgements, when united, is ftronger; fo the right of exercifing them becomes, by their union, ftronger likewife. For feparate rights, being joined together, confirm and ftrengthen each other. The rights of individuals confifting of fo many units, when collected into one general fum, that fum muft be equal to all its parts; and greater than any leffer number of them. Therefore the right of the aggregate body muft be greater than that of the individuals which form it, not only taken fingly,

but

but than all of them in their feparate capacities.

Apply this to the community. Whatever right of private judgement fingle
members of it have; thefe rights, being
accumulated, grow ftronger, and more
perfect. If a private perfon may frame
rules for his private conduct; the publick
furely may do the fame—may make laws
for itfelf—for the well-ordering of its
own government; that is, for every member
of it, binding every one.

If there be a right of private judgement;
this, in fociety, muft be productive of a
right of publick judgement. For there
furely is fuch a thing as publick judgement, as well as private; and the one hath
its rights no lefs than the other: Nay, it
is becaufe there is a right of private judgement, that there muft be a right of publick judgement likewife: For the one neceflarily refults from the other. Where
thefe two rights clafh, the weaker muft
neceflarily yield to the ftronger; the private to the publick; muft never interfere

with

with it, unless in very extraordinary cafes, in which compliance would be finful; but muft ordinarily be fuperfeded by it; be governed by its laws, and act in fubordination to it; when that can be done without fin. For it is a firft principle in fociety, that the inclinations of the minority muft be over-ruled by the judgement and decifion of the fuperior number. And it is well-obferved, " that in civil fo- " ciety, compofed, as it commonly is, of " fuch an infinite number of heteroge- " neous and difcordant principles and in- " terefts, in trade, in politicks, and in re- " ligion; where fubjects of contention " prefent themfelves by thoufands every " hour; no conftitution can fubfift a mo- " ment, without a conftant refignation of " private judgement to the judgement of " the publick *." "

The fame reafoning, and the fame principles, will hold good, with regard to civil

---

* Letter from a *Virginian* to the Members of the Congrefs at *Philadelphia.*

and

and ecclefiaftical, fecular and religious rights[x]: Nay, in matters of faith and religion, duly confulted about, if but between two, or three, gathered together in Chrift's name, he himfelf affuredly promifeth his divine prefence, to fuperintend, guide, and direct, their councils[y]. This is more than he hath promifed exprefsly to private judgement; or to confultations feparate from, and efpecially in oppofition to, any publick ones of his church.

[x] Judicium (humanum) ut ad actiones privatas chriftiani cujufque, ita ad publicas actiones, et privatas, quæ publico imperio reguntur, publicarum eft poteftatum; et quidem fummarum in fummo gradu. Vidit hoc jampridem Brentius, cujus hæc funt verba (Proleg.), Ut privatus privatam, ita princeps publicam habet de doctrinâ religionis poteftatem judicandi, et decidendi. Et ita judicio opus eft, præfertim principum, ut fciant quam doctrinam, et privatim ad fuam falutem æternam, et publice in populo Dei tueri debeant.—Grot. de imperio fumm. poteftatum, cap. v. fect. 5.—A treatife, which was written by this great man, in behalf of the Remonftrants, againft thofe in power who oppreffed them.

[y] Matt. xviii. 20.

I hope

I hope it will not be difputed, but that the church of Chrift is a fociety. This appears, in a good meafure, from what hath been obferved already; and that it is, in its defign and conftitution, the moft perfect fociety of all others; having Chrift himfelf for its head; founded by him upon a rock; the moft firmly built, and eftablifhed upon the wifeft laws; and the moft clofely united, and compacted together, in all its parts. This is effential to the nature of the chriftian religion; one of the chief defigns for which it was calculated, being to make human fociety, as well as human nature, perfect. And it militates againft the very temper and genius of it, to engage in any meafures which have a tendency to deftroy or difturb the harmony of the fociety con-ftituted by it.

If therefore the church of Chrift be a fociety, it muft fubfift, as all other fo-cieties do, by the fame general laws of fociety; which are very different from thofe of a ftate of nature, which indeed cannot

cannot properly be said to know scarce any laws at all.

Every man born in society is necessarily abridged much in his natural rights, religious as well as civil. When he comes of age to examine them, he will find himself abridged of them ; and that they had been transferred, by the laws of the constitution, under which he lives, to those who bear rule over him; who, as they judged for him before he was in a capacity of judging for himself; so they go on to judge for him still, in consequence of that right of publick judgement which they have; and of which no man, in his private capacity, can lawfully dispossess them.

The author of the *Confessional* seems to question, whether a man may transfer, or abridge himself, of his right of private judgement [z]: And he treats this, as giving way to an usurpation of Christ's authority; who is King in his own kingdom; and only Lord in matters of conscience;

[z] P. 192. 1st edit.

and

and he afferts, but not proves, that he hath referved this authority to himfelf; and hath delegated no part of it.

But the truth of the cafe is, according to what was juft now obferved, that this right is transferred already; and every man is neceffarily abridged of it, and previoufly to any act or deed of his own, whereby he might either transfer, or retain it; and before he was capable of doing either; and that by the very nature of man, as well as by the laws of fociety; whereby no man was ever in actual poffeffion of this right at his firft fetting out in life. For we all get into poffeffion of it gradually, as we grow in underftanding; whereby we are enabled to exercife it. For he needs not be told, that there is a time when we are not capable of judging for ourfelves: And will this gentleman call it an invafion of the right of private judgement, or an ufurpation of Chrift's authority, in others, under whofe care we are placed, to judge for us under that incapacity?

Even

Even this learned author himfelf, poffeffed of a good natural judgement, as he
certainly is, to an eminent degree, improved by ftudy and application, and ri-
pened by years and experience, feems, in
the very inftance which he is judging |
about, to be rather diffident of his own
judgement; as he makes it a queftion,
which he leaves undetermined, Whether
he can transfer, or abridge himfelf of, his
right to ufe it for himfelf?

With regard to the authority of Chrift
our Lord and King, he doth not exercife
it here any otherwife than inwardly by
his Spirit, and outwardly in his word;
and by the overfeers and governors of his
church. Thefe powers are very confiftent with each other[a]. And that he
hath

[a] Summum Chrifti judicium, huic de quo agimus
judicio, (nempe judicio fummarum poteftatum circa
facra) non magis repugnat, quam ejufdem imperium,
fummarum poteftatum imperio; quod fupra oftendiffe
fatis eft. Legiflatio præmium pœnamque æternam vi
fuâ ferens, et ex eâ lege ultima judicatio, folius eft
Chrifti. Medio tempore interfatur Chiftus per Spi-
ritum

hath delegated *some part* of his authority
to them, whom he hath appointed to exercife it, is fufficiently plain, and cannot
be contefted with any fhew of argument,
from the folemn inveftiture and delivery
of the keys; which are enfigns and em-
blems of authority ; and this repeatedly
confirmed by exprefs declarations to the
fame effect ᵇ. The contrary opinion is that
of the *Fifth-monarchy men,* which I hope
is not going to be revived.

We are initiated into Chrift's kingdom
by baptifm, and made his difciples, and
fubjects, by his minifters. During our
minority, we are under tutors and governors, in our religious, as well as civil capacities. Being fuppofed by the law not
fit to judge and act for ourfelves, in either
refpect, we have others appointed to judge
and act for us. When we grow up, we

ritum fuum judicio divino; neque tamen fequitur id
judicium actio humana, nifi intercedente judicio hu-
mano. Grot. ib. fub titulo, Non obftare (judicio fummarum poteftatum circa facra), quod Chriftus eft
fummus judex.

ᵇ See Matt. xvi. 19. — xviii. 18. John xx. 23.

continue

continue to have paſtors and teachers; from whom we are ſuppoſed to imbibe our religious principles; and to be farther taught and guided by, in the knowledge and practice of Chriſtianity. And many, too many, notwithſtanding all the inſtruction they receive, are but poorly qualified to exerciſe their right of private judgement, in this reſpect, as long as they live. Not only the ignorant and illiterate, but many others of competent knowledge and learning, ſubmit themſelves to the guidance of others—of thoſe particularly, whoſe profeſſion and office is ſuppoſed to qualify them for ſuch a truſt; and that not merely out of indolence and indifference; but often on account of other occupations, other ſtudies and profeſſions; and out of a modeſt diffidence of their own judgements; and a becoming ſubmiſſion and deference to the judgements of ſuch, as they, on good probability, preſume are better able to judge for them, than they are for themſelves [c].

[c] Vide Grot. *ib.* p. 228.

And

And thus they may be said to repose a kind of implicit faith in the judgement of the church; even of the proteftant church under which they live. Let not any one be ftartled at the expreffion. There is a great difference between the *making* of fuch a faith neceffary, by keeping the people in ignorance; and its *becoming* neceffary by their own neglect, or incapacity; or otherwife expedient, by a voluntary and confidential repofal of it. And there will be more or lefs of this latter in all proteftant, as well as popifh countries, in proportion as men continue ignorant, and incapable, and fatisfied with it: And till it wears off, the beft expedient to fupply the want of an explicit faith, or knowledge, is the teaching of faithful paftors in the doctrines of a found and orthodox church. And perhaps it would be much better, as well for their real edification, as for the peace and unity of the church, if the people would be content with fuch teaching; rather than to fwerve from it, and *turn-afide into vain jangling*;

whence

whence they come to such a pass, as *not to endure found doctrine* ; but having *itching ears, heap to themselves teachers, who under-stand neither what they say, nor whereof they affirm* ; *deceiving and being deceived* [d].

Thus people set up to judge for themselves, before they are duly qualified for it: No wonder therefore they so often judge amiss. It is a premature, and *injudicious* use of their own *judgement*, not tempered with humility, which misleads them. When they acquire more true christian knowledge, they will be less conceited; and less liable to be *toffed to and fro, and carried about with every wind of doctrine, by the fleight of men, and cunning craftiness, whereby they lie in wait to deceive* [e].

On the other hand, the doctrine and practice of implicit faith was so shamefully imposed upon its vaffals by the church of *Rome*, that it was high time for people to open their eyes, and to judge for themselves ; when they found they

[d] 2 Tim. iv. 3. — iii. 13.   [e] Eph. iv. 14.

had

had been fo much abufed by it, and it had been made the vehicle of the moft grofs, monftrous, and abfurd impofitions.

Many of thofe who had emancipated themfelves from its fhackles, held this doctrine in fuch difdain, and were fo jealous of it, that they thought they could hardly run far enough from it; and therefore never ftopt till they got into the contrary extreme. And now this is generally looked upon as a bug-bear, quite banifhed from among all found proteftants; and fcarce known to have fhelter any where out of the church of *Rome*. They think no quarter ought to be given it; and any one, who fhould offer a word in its behalf, would perhaps be charged, by the author of the *Confeffional*, as *edging* towards popery.

Notwithftanding, I muft own myfelf fo much a *papift*, as to fay for *implicit faith*, that there is, and ever will be, much of it in the world, whether we will or no. It creeps into every department of life in fpite of us. It is neceffary to the very

necef-

neceffaries of it. We can neither eat,
drink, nor fleep, without it : Neither can
we keep it out of the church, or conven-
ticle.

It may not here be improper to fpeak a
word, or two, to the cafe of youth being
required to fubfcribe to the *Thirty-nine articles of religion*, at their matriculation into
the univerfity of *Oxford.*

Thefe young perfons are generally in a
ftate of minority ; and are not deemed, by
the laws of their country, to have difcretion enough for the management of their
own fecular affairs. The municipal law of
the univerfity is, in this refpect, perfectly
conformable to the law of the land in general: And is it not fit it fhould be fo?
It cannot be expected they fhould be better
qualified to judge of abftrufe points in divinity, than of the propriety of laying out
their own money. They have been hitherto under guardians and tutors : They
are neceffarily fo ftill. Are they notwithftanding defirous of knowing what they
fubfcribe ? and refolved to ftudy and weigh

H every

every article, before they signify their af-
sent and consent to it in writing? If so,
they are quite in the right. They are
much to be commended, .and by all means
to be encouraged and affisted in their enquiries. If they meet with any unfur-
mountable difficulties, which they cannot
submit to the determination of their supe-
riors, let them with-hold their hands, and
be content to turn their backs, without
subscribing at all, until they are better fatisfied. No body compels them to subscribe: But if they think fit to acquiesce
in the judgement of the learned body, into
which they are going to be incorporated;
they may safely subscribe these articles,
though they may not understand them,
nor have ever read them: And this they
may do in the fame implicit manner, as
they do in a thousand other instances.
The articles may be considered, as an ini-
tiating lecture, or as the foundation of a
course of lectures; which it is proper they
should pay the like attention to, as to the
subsequent lectures delivered to them, both
publick

publick and private. And if it is not un-
fuitable to the ſtate of grown perſons, as
men and chriſtians, to pay a proper deference to the doctrine of their teachers,
and to the wiſdom of the church; it is
much more becoming the modeſty and ingenuity of youth, to pay that obedience
of their underſtanding to thoſe, of whom
they come to learn.

Such ſtudents of the univerſity, as are
deſigned for the miniſtry of the church,
muſt of courſe make theſe articles a part
of their ſtudy, as a neceſſary preparation
for it; their unfeigned aſſent and conſent
to the doctrines contained in them being
what they will be again required to ſignify
in writing, in order to their admiſſion into
the miniſtry; and then they are ſuppoſed
to do it more explicitly. And I will not
diſſemble my wiſhes, that the *Thirty-nine*
articles of religion, and divinity in general,
were more ſtudied, and lectured upon, both
in publick and private, than I doubt they
are, in both univerſities. Young men
would not then come ſo poorly qualified,

when

when they offer themfelves for holy orders, as, I fpeak from experience, I have
been too often grieved to find them.

   As matters ftand, fufficient time is allowed ftudents in both univerfities to per-
ufe and weigh the purport of the articles; and either to proceed in their defign,
or betake themfelves to other callings, or
profeffions, if they fcruple fubfcribing to
them. For this is required by our church
of none, but members of the univerfity,
clergymen, or minifters, and fchool-mafters; though other churches have extended this teft much farther.

   Fuller obferves, that in the church of
England, "no lay perfon," except as above,
" was required to fubfcribe; no magi-
" ftrate; none of the commons, according
" to the feverity in other places. For the
" perfecuted church of the *Englifh* in
" *Frankford,* in Queen *Mary's* days, de-
" manded fubfcription to their difcipline
" of every man, yea even of women:
" And the *Scotch,* in the minority of
" King *James,* exacted it of noblemen,
                                " gentlemen,

" gentlemen, and courtiers; which here
" was extended only to men of ecclefi-
" aftical functions[f]." And the holy difcipline of the *Puritans* here in *England*
enjoined, " That every one, as well men
" as women, which defired to be received
" into their congregation, fhould make a
" declaration, or confeffion of their faith,
" before the minifters, and elders, fhewing
" himfelf fully to confent and agree with
" the doctrine of the church; and fub-
" mitting themfelves to the difcipline of
" the fame; and the fame to teftify, by
" fubfcribing thereto, if they can write[s]."
And every member of the congregation
was obliged to render a declaration of his
faith before the minifters and elders,
whenever they thought fit to require it:
Nor were any to be admitted to the communion, without making a confeffion of

[f] *Fuller's* Ecclef. Hift. book ix. p. 72.

[s] Bifhop *Maddock's* Anfwer to *Neale*, p. 51. The
quotation is in the words of the original, the gram-
maticalnefs of which I will not anfwer for.

their

their faith, and submitting themselves to the discipline.

From this comparative view, none can help acknowledging the moderation of the church of *England* in this respect.

But the author of the *Confessional* disputes the right of establishing confessions of faith at all[h]: And denies, that the church hath any authority to require subscription to articles of faith, or religion[i].

Its authority in this respect may be defended even upon the principle of the right of private judgement itself. For if every private christian hath a right to judge for himself; every christian society must have this right, *a fortiori*. Though, if we distinguish properly in this case, it was by the prince, that learned divines in the church were ordered and authorized, to draw up its articles; and it was by his authority, or rather by that of the whole legislature, including church and state, that subscription was, and is, required to

[h] P. 31.   [i] P. 88.

be

be made to them: And this fubfcription is made a condition of holding preferment by the ftate, as well as the church.

Indeed, this gentleman difputes the authority of the one, as well as the other, for requiring any fuch fubfcription; in whom we have an inftance of a church of *England* man agreeing with papifts and diffenters, in denying princes the authority of making laws in church-matters. But I hope every prince, either by himfelf, or in conjunction with thofe who fhare the government with him, hath power to enact laws, for the well-ordering of that government, with which he is entrufted: And the articles of the church of *England* are part of the law of the land; to which the fame regard fhould be paid, as to the other parts of it; and it is as reafonable to plead exemption from the one, as the other.

A man, to qualify himfelf for civil offices, muft take fuch and fuch oaths; for ecclefiaftical functions, he muft fubfcribe a certain body of articles. If he fcruple to take fuch oaths, he gives up all thoughts of fuch office: And if he fcruple fub-fcribing thofe articles, fhould he not be content to drop the funčtion?

This is a preliminary condition to be complied with. Every man undoubtedly may, and ought to think for himfelf, in his private capacity. But no private man can go farther. If he afpire to act in a publick capacity, he muft fubmit to the laws appointed by the publick—by thofe who are invefted with publick authority in that refpect; of whatever nature his employment be, whether ecclefiaftical or civil: The fame rule of conduct fhould be obferved in the church, as in the ftate, in religious, as in civil concerns.

Every fociety likewife hath furely a natural right to do every thing neceffary to its own prefervation; in which general right is included that of beftowing offices. Thus a number of travellers have a right to chufe for themfelves a guide for their journey: A number of voyagers, a pilot

for

for their ſhip: And a free nation hath a right to chuſe a king [k].

Hence it follows, that every ſociety hath a right of preſcribing the conditions, on which, and on which alone, it beſtows its offices, and every thing elſe relating to them. The church of *England*, as a ſociety, beſtows the office of teaching, and adminiſtering the word and ſacraments, upon condition of ſubſcribing to her articles of faith and religion : And herein ſhe requires no more than what ſhe hath a natural right to require, according to the above argument; by which alone ſuch requiſition is ſufficiently juſtified.

But moreover, the depriving her of this right would be depriving her of a privilege, which every private chriſtian hath a claim to—the privilege of judging for herſelf. The

[k] Thus argues *Grotius*. Naturaliter cœtui unicuique permittitur ea procurare, quæ ad conſervationem ſui ſunt neceſſaria : In quo numero eſt functionum applicatio. Ita viatores multi jus habent eligendi gubernatorem ſuæ navis; viatores itineris ducem; populus liber regem. Grot. ib. cap. x. ſect. 3.

church,

church, the body of chriftians in general, in their publick and collective capacity, is denied that privilege by fome of her members, which they daily exercife themfelves without referve, in publick, as well as private.

They likewife deny her the privilege of expreffing her own fenfe of fcripture in her own words; which if they themfelves were denied, we fhould not fail to hear fuch an unreafonable reftraint laid upon chriftian liberty, loudly, and indeed juftly remonftrated againft. They will fubmit to no *human explanations* of fcripture—to no *human creeds,* or articles of faith whatfoever. But every explanation, or interpretation, which the church makes, muft be expreffed in the words of fcripture only [1]. Would they themfelves fubmit to this injunction which they want to lay upon her? Would they be willing, or even able to bear it? Since they take upon them to prefcribe laws to the church, they fhould at leaft be well affured of the practicability

[1] In this they have the countenance of the old *Levelers;* who would allow of no argument from fcripture, but in the exprefs words of fcripture itfelf.

of

of them. Let them therefore, to this
end, try the experiment firſt themſelves,
and apply the rule of expreſſing their ſenſe
of ſcripture in none but ſcripture-words,
to their own practice; which it is but fair
they ſhould do; and they will ſoon find
what wretched work they would make of
it. They will be as ready to lay it aſide,
as *David* was to put off *Saul's* armour,
which he had not proved.

Scripture is undoubtedly the beſt in-
terpreter of ſcripture, as far as it will
go; and *ſpiritual things* are beſt *compared
with ſpiritual.* But farther explanations are
often neceſſary; in which, from the nature of the thing, a latitude of expreſſion
muſt be made uſe of: Otherwiſe our liberty will be ſo cramped, that we ſhall
every now and then be at a loſs how to
expreſs ourſelves; and all the latitude poſ-
ſible is often little enough to convey our
own ſenſe with clearneſs and preciſion;
and to guard againſt miſapprehenſion and
cavil. If we keep to the ſenſe of ſcripture, and the analogy of faith, the mode
of expreſſion can be attended with no ill

4   conſe-

confequences; otherwife the very letter of fcripture, in bad, or unfkilful hands, might be turned againft itfelf.

The *Confeffional* furnifhes us with inftances of the *Calvinifts* charging the *Remonftrants* with cherifhing the worft meanings under fcripture-words; and of the *Remonftrants* bringing the fame accufation againft another fet of men [m].

If this rule of rejecting all human explanations, and fticking to the words of fcripture only, were always obferved, the province of divinity would lie within a very narrow compafs; and an infinite variety and profufion of books, and learned labour would be faved. There would be an end of teaching, and preaching; nor would there be any room left for writing on this, or any other fubject in divinity; we would have nothing to do, but to read our bibles; and, if no human creeds are allowed of, we fhall not have fo much as the apoftle's creed left us.

[m] P. 75.

For

For what ends then are fuch rigid terms prefcribed to the framers of confeffions, and articles of faith, but to tie up their hands, that all others may be free from any reftraint upon their principles? This is plainly no more than a fubterfuge, to evade the fubfcribing of any confeffion, or articles of faith whatfoever. If thefe reformers are to have their wills, and to go on at this rate, how much of our Chriftianity will they leave us?

With the like view, fyftems of divinity have been much inveighed againft, and fyftematical divines have been arraigned; in general terms indeed, but in fuch terms, as if there were fomething monftrous in them; and as if they were pregnant with I know not what mifchief. But is there any thing fo very bad in fyftems, and the writers of them, as fuch? A fyftem of any fcience is a methodical combination and arrangement of parts, concurring to make one confiftent whole: And a fyftem of divinity is, in other words, no more than a confiftent body of divinity. And

ſhould

fhould it not be fuch? Should not every whole be fo fitly framed together, as to have the concurrence and confent of all its parts confpiring to the formation of it? Without which, it would be fuch a motley and ridiculous piece, as the poet defcribes

ut nec pes, nec caput uni

Reddatur formæ ——— cui uxus et alter

Affuitur pannus ———

I hope the holy fcripture will be allowed to be confiftent with itfelf in all its parts. Therefore furely it is poffible a confiftent fcheme of *agenda et credenda* may be drawn from it. The Ten Commandments are a fyftem of moral duties. Are they the worfe for that? The Apoftles Creed contains a fyftem of truths to be believed, not indeed in fcripture terms, *totidem verbis*; yet in fubftance to be found there. Is this the reafon why that, and call other creeds, are condemned? There were creeds before there were any written gofpels; for we find references to, and recitals of, fome fhort formularies of this kind

kind in the gospels, themselves. I hope they will let us have them.

I own there may have been systems of divinity so clumsily drawn up, and so awkwardly put together, as not to harmo-nize with themselves; and glaring con-tradictions might perhaps be found in them. Some likewise may contain doc-trines that are inconsistent with the ana-logy of faith. Let such, if such there be, be pointed out, and rejected. But let not all systematical, and regular writings be condemned in the lump, for the sake of them. Systematical writers are much disdained, for their being narrow-minded, and too much cramped and confined in their notions. Their notions, I presume, are grounded upon scripture, by which their minds are limited; and within which I am sure they may find room enough to expatiate. If others contend for trans-gressing these bounds, to themselves be it. *We have no such custom, nor the churches of God.*

I wish

I wish such confiderations as these may contribute to 'overcome that averfion, which many have conceived againft fyftems in general; and plead fo far in their behalf, that they may have fair quarter given them. For it is with no particular view to the church of *England*, any otherwife than as it is a branch of the catholick church of Chrift, profeffing a confiftent fet of doctrines, that I have offered this apology for fyftems of divinity; which are alone quarreled with. For I do not find, that fyftems in other fciences are at all difapproved of; a fhrewd fign that there is fomething worfe at bottom; which this is but a veil for.

To what hath been faid concerning the right of private judgement, it may not be amifs to add a few confiderations on the *exercife* of that right.

And here furely fome *decorum* fhould be obferved in this refpect; fome regard paid by individuals to the whole body; and fome degree of veneration fhould be reckoned due from private chriftians, in

judging

judging for themfelves, to the judgement of thofe *who bear rule over them, and watch for their fouls, attending continually on this very thing.*

The exercife of private judgement is not only the right, but the duty of all chriftians, as far as they have it in their power; that they may be able to *give a reafon of the hope that is in them.*

But let them at the fame time remember, that this judgement of theirs is *private*; in virtue of which, they can have no right, or pretence, to dictate to others — much lefs to the church in general — and much lefs ftill fhould they fet up their own judgements in oppofition to hers — to thwart and contradict it — difdain all deference to her judgement; and affume fuch a felf-fufficiency, as fets itfelf above all government and control.

Every good chriftian, and every peaceable member of fociety, in the exercife of his private judgement, how far foever he is capable of carrying it, will put the moft favourable conftruction upon doctrines and

I   ordi-

ordinances, grown venerable by age ; and long ago eſtabliſhed by lawful authority. He will endeavour to bring his own ſentiments into a conformity to them, as far as is conſiſtent with the clear dictates of reaſon and ſcripture. He will be more inclined, when doubts ariſe, to ſuſpect ſome error in his own apprehenſions, ſome fallacy in his own reaſonings, than in deciſions grounded on ſuch reſpectable ſanctions. He will proceed with the utmoſt caution ; and will get the beſt information he can have, for the ſolving of his doubts and difficulties. He will add prayer to ſtudy ; and beſeech God to illuminate his underſtanding, rectify his errors, and to grant him a right apprehenſion, in this, and all other reſpects. And if, after all his endeavours, he finds himſelf under a neceſſity of differing in judgement from his ſuperiors, he will keep his ſentiments to himſelf; unleſs he thinks it will be more for the good of religion to divulge them : In which caſe, he will do it with modeſty, deference, and

openneſs

opennefs to conviction; *not contentious, heady, high-minded*—not *defpifing government,* nor *prefumptuous, and felf-willed;* but *afraid to fpeak evil of dignities*[n]. Though he be ever fo fully perfuaded in his own mind ; he will caft down his own reafonings, rather than deftroy the unity, or difturb the peace, of the church. That charity which he owes to all mankind, he will think is more efpecially due to the eftablifhed church—that charity, which *beareth all things, believeth all things, hopeth all things, endureth all things*[o].

He will confider, that under a free and fettled government, every man is fuppofed to have given his confent, either exprefsly, or tacitly, by himfelf, or his reprefentatives, to all its laws and injunctions ; and that there is but one, and the fame rule to judge by, in all cafes, relating to all the parts of it, in church and ftate : And as in the ftate we are to fubmit to all its laws, enacted by lawful authority, which are

[n] 2 Tim. iii. 4.   2 Pet. ii. 10.
[o] 1 Cor. xiii. 7.

agree-

agreeable to its conſtitution; and have a tendency to preſerve, and not to over-throw, and deſtroy it: So in the church, while her antient conſtitution is preſerved; and no innovations in doctrine, nor in-croachments of power, are made, or at-tempted; here the ſubject hath no cauſe to complain; nor any pretence to with-draw his ſubmiſſion, or exerciſe his right of private judgement; ſo far as to diſturb the peace of the church; to excite jea-louſies; or foment diviſions in, or ſepara-tions from her.

The church of *England* cannot be juſtly charged with any attempts of theſe kinds. With regard to doctrine, it hath been al-ready obſerved, that it is invariably the ſame, as it was, when firſt ſettled at the Reformation; no formal alterations having been made in it; nor any conſiderable de-parture from it; whatever hath been the caſe with regard to individuals; who may have held opinions different from, or con-trary to, the eſtabliſhed faith and doc-trine; which are not to be placed to her
account,

account, as long as the foundation laid in
her articles, conformably to fcripture,
ftandeth fure ; and fhe holds faft the profeffion of them.

With regard to power, the *moderation*
of our church *is known unto all men,* and
is often praifed by foreigners, and others,
who are not of her communion. Her government is fo far from making any en-
croachments ; that it is neceffarily reftrained, in the exercife of difcipline, and
all outward jurifdiction, by her being incorporated with the ftate. This want of
a ftricter difcipline is often lamented by
her beft friends, and the reftoration of it is
much wifhed for by herfelf [P]. But that is
become the lefs practicable, on account of
her powers having been farther abridged by
the toleration. The exemption of fuch
numerous bodies from her jurifdiction, is
what fhe hath little caufe to regret, as it
renders her burden the lighter : But it is
matter of real grief and concern to her,
that too many libertines, within her own
bofom, are ready enough to take advantage

[P] See the Commination-office.

I 3   from

from hence, for fpurning at her authority, and bidding defiance to her laws; as they know they have an eafy way to evade them. Hence her cenfures are in a great meafure laid afide, or otherwife are difregarded. Her laws are not carried into execution; and are encroached upon by prohibitions from the temporal courts: And the convocation never fits now to do bufinefs. This hath expofed her to the infults, not only of fuch as are without; but even of her own gremial fons; thofe who eat of her bread, lifting up their heel againft her,

On the other hand, we have reafon to be thankful to the Divine Providence, and under it, to our governors in church and ftate, for having preferved to our church the privileges, which fhe doth ftill enjoy. If fhe is deprived of any of her original powers; fhe efcapes the *odium* of exercifing them: And if in fome things fhe is over-ruled by the ftate; fhe derives, from her coalition with it, the fupport, ftrength, and ftability, of the common conftitution.

The

The controverfy, fo warmly debated, at the end of the laft, and beginning of the prefent century, about the rights and privileges of the convocation, though it then produced nothing but heat, and a fufpenfion of thofe very rights and privileges; yet they have been the better cleared up, and afcertained, by this controverfy; and it ferves as a caution to all future convocations, when their deliberations are called for, to obferve greater temper in their debates. And it is hoped the time is not very diftant, when the wifdom of government may fee reafon for a convocation to tranfact bufinefs; which will be of the higheft importance and benefit to this church; if properly conducted, and brought to a happy iffue.

If the coercive powers of the church are reftrained, fhe enjoys the powers of perfuafion in their full force; which are derived from a higher authority, and favour of the primitive fimplicity of paftoral power. And thefe fpiritual powers, when properly exerted, carry fuch force and energy

I 4

energy with them, as renders the exercife
of any temporal power the lefs neceffary;
and the want of it to be the lefs regretted.

It is not to be diffembled, that our difcipline is fallen into fo relaxed a ftate, as
not to be many removes from *Eraftianifm*.
Yet even this hath its advantages, as we
have partly feen: To which may be added,
that the imputation of an enflaving, tyrannical, hierarchy cannot, with any juftice,
be applicable to our church at prefent,
whatever it might have been heretofore;
though it is as liberally applied to her
now, as if fhe were in the *zenith* of her
power, and enforced it with the utmoft ri-
gour.   Indeed, an hierarchy, as fuch, hath
nothing tyrannical, or even arbitrary, in
the idea of it.   The title is venerable; it
being a government *in facris*, adminiftered
by perfons of a facerdotal character; which
therefore the church of *England* hath a
juft claim to, though it was never affected by her. And if ufed only by way of
diftinction from prefbyterian, or rather independent, government, which is partly
2   admi-

adminiftered by laymen, it hath nothing improper or invidious in it. But this fa-cred government having been abufed by the church of *Rome* to the worft of pur-pofes, ufurping *dominion over men's faith, and lording it over God's heritage,* in a moft cruel and tyrannical manner, the idea of defpotick power was transferred to the hierarchy of the church of *England,* by thofe who were difaffected towards her; and the imputation, however unde-fervedly, hath been induftrioufly propa-gated ever fince.

The church of *England* difclaims all pretenfions to fupremacy; and acknow-ledges the King's Majefty to be, under Chrift, the fupreme head of the church, as well as of the ftate. This acknow-ledgement is founded in the *act* of fub-miffion, made to King *Henry* VIII, which continued in force during the reign of *Edward* VI, and was revived 1 *Elizabeth.* An oath was framed in recognition of this fupremacy; and enjoined to be taken by all officers and minifters, ecclefiaftical and

and civil. The *thirty-feventh article* of religion agrees with this oath ; and fo do
the *canons* of 1603. Our church teaches
obedience to be paid, by all orders and
ranks of men, to our Sovereign Lord the
King: And the government which fhe
claims, and exercifes, is only a fubordi-
nate one, for the more regular and decent
provifion for, and obfervation of, the divine worfhip, and ordinances ; and for the
neceffary maintenance of order and difcipline. She fets up no *imperium in imperio,* to thwart, or curb, the civil government ; as the church of *Rome* doth in
countries fubjeﬅ to her—makes no en-
croachments on the laws of the ﬅate, nor
clafhes with it in any refpeﬅ. She holds
no principles inimical to, nor derogatory
from, the fecular government ; and main-
tains fuch only, as are conformable to it,
and contribute to its fupport. The law of
the church, is the civil and canon law, interpreted, and carried into execution, not by
clergymen, but civilians ; who prefide over,
and occupy, her courts ; and almoﬅ all
the

the ecclesiastical courts of the kingdom are kept by laymen.

This, indeed, hath been urged, as one of the principal objections against the government of our church. But it comes with no good grace from those, who place so much of their discipline in the hands of lay persons, not professing the law, nor ordinarily distinguished by any superior qualifications for their office. The bishops are censured for devolving so much of their power upon their chancellors; and yet the hierarchy is thought to have too much power still. In the days of popish ignorance, few, besides the clergy, had much knowledge of the law; and they bare a great sway in our courts of law, in general[q]; the people being kept in ignorance of that, as well as all other branches of science. When learning began to be cultivated; the study of the law, being so

[q] Antiently the masters of chancery, and of the rolls; the clerks in chancery, and of the exchequer; were all clergymen. And the clerks of the King's courts, and of parliament, were clergymen also.

useful

ufeful a part of it, was not neglected.
This by degrees became a diftinct profeffion; and our courts of law were occupied by laymen, in proportion as they became learned in it. The clergy, of courfe,
were then lefs wanted in that department;
and the Reformation taking place, there
was fufficient employment for them in
promoting it; and in the more proper
ftudies and duties of their function, in
confequence of it; which in truth continue to be the moft proper for them ftill.
They therefore withdrew from the ftudy
and practice of the civil law, which,
ftrictly fpeaking, was foreign to their profeffion: Or, rather, they gave place to
thofe, who devoted themfelves to this
particular fcience; and who therefore are
juftly deemed to be the beft fkilled in it;
and beft qualified to adminifter and difpenfe
it. Their merit of courfe entitles them to
the emoluments of it. And they undoubtedly would think it an injurious en-
croachment, if the clergy were now to
rival them in it.

The:e

There is nothing intolerant in the conftitution of the church of *England*; and *Rapin*, a profeffed prefbyterian, doth her the juftice to acknowledge, " that he doth " not find in her principles, or doctrines, " any thing repugnant to charity, or " tending to violence '."

The prefbyterian government is much extolled for its mildnefs and moderation; its principles of liberty and popularity; and its freedom from the fhackles of churchmen. This government was once eftablifhed over this nation; and from the teft of experience, the fureft of all others, we have no reafon to admire it fo much, in preference to that of the church of *England*.

If we examine that platform of difcipline, which was long fo ftrenuoufly contended for; and which at length prevailed to be fet up, upon the ruins of the church of *England*; and was exercifed for a while; we fhall foon be convinced of the difference between them; and perceive,

' *Rapin's* Hift. of England, 1632.

which

which hath the beſt title to meekneſs, and moderation; and which is to be thought the more arbitrary and tyrannical; and even ſeditious, and dangerous to government.

This diſcipline, in an account given of it, extracted from the writings of the *Puritans* themſelves, who lived under the reign of Queen *Elizabeth*, appears to have had a manifeſt tendency to the overthrow of her Majeſty's government and prerogative, as well in cauſes civil, as 021 ecclefiaſtical, in the following inſtances, among many others—In depriving her Majeſty of all right to patronage in the church— By claiming the laſt appeal, and the ſupreme authority, in all cauſes and matters ecclefiaſtical—By making her Majeſty ſubject to the cenſures, and excommunications of their elderſhips, and other aſſemblies—By authorizing certain magiſtrates, even to depoſe their ſovereign, either by war, or otherwiſe, if he ſeemed to them to break covenant—By teaching that the government of the commonwealth muſt

be

be framed to the government of the church; whereby it muſt of courſe be made republican. They farther claimed an immunity of the revenues of perſons eccleſiaſtical, from publick impoſitions. They were for abrogating, or changing, the greateſt part of the laws of the land. They arraigned the juſtice of the realm; and diſdained the authority of the chriſtian magiſtrate.

Theſe, and many other dangerous doctrines, and enormous claims, they boldly taught, and peremptorily inſiſted upon; even threatening they ſhould prevail, in ſpight of the Queen and council, and all that oppoſed them: And they proved as good as their word. For they adhered ſo cloſely to their plan, that they perſevered in urging it, during the beſt part of three long reigns, for the ſpace of above eighty years; when at length they carried it into execution with a vengeance; and put it in practice, in the whole, and every part, attended with ſuch

conſefequences, as are too well known, and too painful to relate [*].

Rapin's account of the principles of his friends, the *Prefbyterians,* is not much more favourable, than the foregoing one. But his character of their own offspring, the *Independents,* is much worfe. He fays, " Their principles were very proper " to put the kingdom in a flame, as they " did effectually.   With regard to the " ftate, they abhorred monarchy; and ap- " proved only of a republican govern- " ment.   And as to religion, their prin- " ciples," he fays, " were contrary to thofe " of all the reft of the world.   They " were not only averfe to epifcopacy; but " would not fo much as endure ordinary " minifters in the church.   They main- " tained, every man might pray in pub- " lick, exhort his brethren, interpret the

---

[*] See *Strype's* Life of Archbifhop *Whitgift,* Appendix to Book iv. N° iii; where what hath been here advanced may be feen more at large, in one view; with references to the writings of thofe Puritans, from which the whole was extracted, by the author [of *Foxes and Firebrands.*

" fcrip-

" fcriptures, according to the talents God
" had endowed him with. It was the
" particular intereft of thefe men fo to
" manage, that the government of the
" ftate fhould be changed, or rather over-
" thrown ; well knowing their party could
" never fubfift, but in anarchy ʹ."

This

ʹ The diffenters now are moftly *Independents* ; but,
I hope, are become more moderate in their principles.
The laws that were made againft them, in general,
after the Reftoration, *Rapin* acknowledges, were neceffary to the church of *England*, for felf-prefervation ;
as they were always irreconcilable enemies to it ; and
their principles tended to the utter ruin of it ; which
they aimed at, in order to change it for their own
difcipline. And, unlefs they fhew themfelves better
difpofed towards it, it is humbly fubmitted to the
wifdom of the legiflature, whether it would not be ftill
proper to keep thofe laws in force, by way of precau-
tion, and *in terrorem ?* Nor can they complain, that
any other ufe hath been made of them ; as, I believe,
they cannot produce a fingle inftance of their having,
in thefe times, been put in execution againft them.
See *Rapin ib. ad ann.* 1640, and 1644-5.

The reader may obferve, that, throughout this treatife, the authors that are quoted, againft the diffenters,
are generally fuch as are of their own perfuafion ;

K think

This retrospect, I own, goes beyond the design of these papers: Nor should it ever have appeared, had it not been in a manner extorted, by the panegyricks, which I see are now publishing, on the characters and merits of those presbyterian and independent divines, whose real principles are here briefly delineated—A publication, which can answer no end, but to irritate and enflame; and to revive grievances, which, on all hands, had been better buried in oblivion[u]. This plainly betrays a working of the old leven out anew; and ill accompanies any solicitations for farther indulgence, to a spirit, which forebodes no good use that is likely to be made of it, in case it should be granted. I hope I may be excused, for stepping thus far out of my way; to animadvert upon a design, so contrary to that of these papers.

think favourably of them; or at least are moderate churchmen. And that the authority of all high-church writers is studiously avoided, unless recourse is sometimes had to it, for the proof of facts.

[u] See the Non-conformists memorial, now publishing in numbers.

To

To proceed. Nearly allied to the queftion concerning the right of private
judgement, is that relating to chriftian liberty; or liberty of confcience, as it is
called : By which, I fuppofe, is meant,
the liberty of following the dictates of
confcience, in all the outward acts of religious worfhip. For confcience itfelf is
very fafe; nor can any force be put upon
it, with regard to its inward feelings and
fenfations; which it is always at perfect
liberty to attend to.

Mr. *Locke*, in the preface to his letters
on toleration, hath thefe words— " Ab-
" folute liberty, juft and true liberty,
" equal and impartial liberty, is the thing
" which we ftand in need of." This notion of liberty, entertained by fo great a
man, the author of the *Confeffional*, and
his followers, have not failed to avail
themfelves of; and they have extended it
much farther, I am perfuaded, than Mr.
Locke ever intended. *Abfolute* liberty is
not only romantick and enthufiaftical in
the notion of it; but it is inconfiftent

K 2   with

with thofe other conditions, of its being *juſt* and *true,* *equal* and *impartial*; and would be even deſtructive of itſelf. For a ſtate of abſolute liberty would be a ſtate of anarchy and confuſion; in which every man would do what would be right in his own eyes, and would be making his own will law; the conſequence of which would be, that we ſhould have neither law, nor liberty. Every man would be encroaching on the liberty of his neighbour. The weak would become a prey to the ſtrong; and the many, ſlaves to a few; and thofe the worſt among them. Even thefe would be ſlaves too—ſlaves to the greateſt tyrants of all others—to their own tyrannous luſts and paſſions. Infomuch that, if mankind were indulged with liberty to the extent implied in the term *abſolute,* they could not contrive how they might be deprived of it more effectually. And, if theré are any ſuch, whom nothing lefs than abſolute liberty will ſatisfy, they muſt go to feek it among the wild *Arabs*; for I am ſure they will

not

not find it in any civilized nation upon earth.

Monfieur *Pufendorff* obferves, " That " an *abfolute* liberty would be fo far from " being ufeful, that it would indeed be. " deftructive to human nature ; and that " therefore the binding and reftraining it, " with laws, is highly conducive to the " good, and to the fafety of mankind." And he obferves farther, " That an abfo- " lute liberty, void of all impediment, " and of all defect, is applicable to God " alone; and is the nobleft attribute of " his fupreme eflence—a perfection, not " only infinite in itfelf, but accompanied " too with infinite power ʷ." And again, " Whoever," fays he, " becomes a ci- " tizen, he refigns up his natural liberty, " and fubjects himfelf to a governing " power ; which includes the right of life " and death ; and at whofe command he " muft confent to do many things, which " he greatly diflikes, and abftain from

ʷ Pufendorff's Law of Nature and Nations, Ch. x.

K 3   " many

" many things which he eagerly de-
" fires [x]."

True and juft liberty confifts in obedience to law; by which it fhould ever be
regulated, as *Cicero* very wifely obferves,
fervi legum ergo fumus, ut liberi effe poffimus [y].
And Mr. *Locke* himfelf elfewhere acknow-
ledges, " That where there is no law,
" there is no freedom." This is far fhort
of *abfolute freedom*, in the ftrict fenfe of
the word; which Mr. *Locke* could never
mean it in: And therefore, as every author ought in candor to be interpreted
by himfelf, he muft be underftood in a
qualified fenfe; but, being rather heated
by his fubject, when he was pleading for
liberty, he let this unguarded expreffion
drop from him; and, under the authority
of his name, it hath been carried to
fuch an extravagant height, as, I dare fay,
he never dreamt of.

[x] Qui civis fit, libertatis naturalis jacturam facit,
et imperio fe fubjicit. Puf. de officio civis, lib. ii.
cap. 5.

[y] Orat. pro Cluentio.

Chriftian

Chriſtian liberty, as well as the right of private judgement, are privileges, which cannot be valued at too high a rate : But theſe are privileges which may be abuſed, by being carried to extremes in the uſe of them : And extremes in the beſt things are always the moſt pernicious. The unhappy diſſentions and diviſions, civil as well as religious, which prevail among us, are melancholy proofs of this great truth ; there being no one cauſe, to which they may more juſtly be imputed, than to the abuſe of theſe privileges : And, if we do not think more ſoberly of ourſelves, in this reſpect, than we are at preſent wont to think ; we may be convinced of our error, when perhaps it will be too late to receive any benefit from the conviction. Poſſibly we may profit by examples drawn from former times. *Liberty of con-ſcience* was the cant word of *Oliver Crom-well*; which he pretended to be very zealous for. We are informed of him, " That " he headed the greateſt part of his army " with *Anabaptiſts, Antinomians, Seekers,*

K 4 " or

" or *Separatifts,* at beft; and that he tied
" them all together, by the point of *li-*
" *berty of confcience*; which was the com-
" mon intereft, wherein they all united.":
And, in defence of it, they contended,
" That the civil magiftrate had nothing
" to do, in matters of religion, by con-
" ftraint, or reftraint; but that every man
" might, not only hold, and believe; but
" preach, and do, in this refpect, what he
" pleafed."

The hiftory of thofe diftracted times
holds out a faithful mirrour to us; in
which, if attentively perufed, we cannot
fail to trace our own likenefs; and dif-
cover the fame latitudinarian principles
coming round again; which, if they grow
upon us, we fhall be as much bewildered
by, as unfettled, as diflocated, and as difu-
nited, as the fectaries of thofe days were;
and likewife as loofe from all religious
principle in reality, as they at laft generally came to be.

z See *Calamy's* Life of *Baxter,* vol. I. p. 54. 90.
99. 110.

Confcious

Confcious however of the neceffity of fome band of union, at leaft in appearance; fubfcription to the fcriptures alone is pro-pofed, as what would anfwer all the in-tents and purpofes of fubfcription what-foever.: Whereas it really would anfwer no other end, than that of an unlimited latitude, which alone is aimed at; fo con-trary to all union, and all the purpofes of it.

For the experience of all ages may teach us, that the fcriptures alone, though all things neceffary and fufficient to falvation are plainly taught in them, yet are not a fufficient prefervative to themfelves, from being mifunderftood, and wrefted, by thofe *that are unlearned, and unftable, unto their own deftruction*[a]. This is what fcripture itfelf informs us of. It is therefore the higheft abfurdity to think, that a vague fubfcription to thefe fame fcriptures fhould be an effectual prefervative againft all thofe falfe doctrines, which have, age after age, been grafted upon them; and fhould

[a] 2 Pet. iii. 16.

alone

alone prove an adequate means of uniting
us in the fame judgement, concerning the
great truths contained in them.

Hence the wifdom of the church hath,
in all ages, found it expedient and neceffary, to guard and fence about them, with
more explicit declarations of fuch doctrines, as fhe perceived were in danger of
being perverted from their juft and primitive fenfe; efpecially if they were fome
of the moft fundamental ones, that were
ftruck at; and, by all the prudent means
in her power, to be watchful over the fa-
cred truft committed to her; and to keep
the word of God from being *corrupted, and*
deceitfully dealt with [b].

But fuppofing fubfcription to the fcriptures alone were to take place—fuppofing
no other teft were required, than a declaration, that a man was "a chriftian and
"a proteftant; and that, as fuch, he re-
"ceived the revelation of the will of God,
"contained in the fcriptures of the Old
"and New Teftament, as the rule of his

----

[b] 2 Cor. ii. 17.—iv. 2.

2   "faith

" faith and practice," would all stand to this test? would this give universal satisfaction?

A considerable body of protestant dissenters soon entered a *caveat* against this test; and prayed to parliament, that the petition for this request might not be granted; alledging, among several other reasons, " that a very great number of pro-
" testant dissenters, ministers, and others,
" would be dissatisfied, if the intended al-
" teration were to take place." And, with regard to those that would be satisfied for the present, are they quite sure, that all would continue long in the same mind?—That some farther alteration in the mode of subscription would not be wanted?—Whether some would not be for refining upon it?—and for making some reserves, some exceptions, and explanations of the sense, in which they subscribed, or declared? They now propose to subscribe in a certain form of words, to be observed by all: Possibly, some may be found, who will

will not subfcribe in any words, but their own.

Dr. *Hartley* difapproved of fubfcribing to the fcriptures at all. " It feems need- " lefs, or enfnaring," fays he, " to fub- " fcribe even to the fcriptures themfelves. " If to any particular canon, or copy, &c. " enfnaring; becaufe of the many real " doubts in thofe things. If not, it is quite " fuperfluous, from the latitude allowed.." And I am really fo far of his mind, that if we are to have no other fubfcription, than fuch a one to the fcriptures, that may as well be let alone; and we may even be without any fubfcription at all.

Many wifh for a new tranflation of the Bible: And fome may fcruple fubfcribing till that is made. But who will enfure a general approbation of it, when it is made? One may be for fubfcribing to this tranflation, and another to that; and fome, to no tranflation, or verfion, at all, antient or modern: But may think it fafeft

^e Effay on Man, vol. ii. p. 353.

to

to go to the fountain-head, and fubfcribe to the fcriptures in their original languages; which, to be fure, they muſt all of courſe be well acquainted with. And ſtill there may be fome, who will not reſt even here. One party may be for fubfcribing to the original *Hebrew*; and be ſticklers for the *Hebrew* verity: While others may give the preference to the *Samaritan Pentateuch.* Some will chuſe to fubfcribe to the *Alexandrian* copy: Some perhaps to the *Vatican*; and fome to neither.

What editions of the original will they all agree to fubfcribe to? Or, is it likely they would come to an agreement about any? It is well known there are many various readings in the ſeveral MSS. of the *Greek Teſtament:* And many likewiſe have of late been difcovered in the *Hebrew* MSS. of the *Old Teſtament.* Who will undertake to furniſh the clue, that ſhall lead us through all this labyrinth! And how many, in the uſe of their own private judgement each, would invariably

follow

follow him throughout? When perfons are feized with fuch a fpirit of refinement, there is no guefling how far it will carry them. Their delicacy is offended at the thoughts of *human* articles, and formularies, and *human* interpretations of fcripture. This others, perhaps, would be apt to call great arrogance, perverfenefs, and felf-fufficiency. Can they fhew us any angelick articles? or direct us to any divine interpretations of the fcriptures; befides what is contained in the fcriptures themfelves?

But while they live among men, they muft fubmit to the common laws of humanity; fomething of which will ftick to them, in fpite of all they can do to diveft themfelves of it: And they muft go out of the world, to be quite free from the impertinence of other people, every now and then interpofing itfelf. The fcriptures were written by men, though dictated by the Spirit of God; and were conveyed down to us by the channel of frail mortals: Nor can they be received, but through the unhallowed hands of fallible

creatures,

creatures; whatever defilements they may be thought to have contracted from them.

I have read of a man, who would not brook the approach of any human inventions to the worſhip, or word of God. This made him cut out of his Bible the contents of the chapters; and the running-titles of the leaves; and thus he reduced it to the bare text, diveſted of binding and cover; though yet he could not, for the life of him, contrive how to diſcharge it of the paper, on which, nor of the ink, with which, it was printed. And this ſame angelick man purſued the principle of ſeparation ſo far, that at length he withdrew from all ſociety with men, leſt he ſhould communicate with them in their ſins. And in this condition he continued, till his children lay dead in the houſe about him; and he became utterly unable to help himſelf[d].

---

[d] Biſhop *Stillingfleet's* ſermon on Phil. iii. 16. From *Ball* againſt *Can.*

What

What now is to be done? We hence plainly fee the neceffity of fome *medium*— fome line to be drawn. I could give fuch refiners a hint to this purpofe, if they could help me to get over one objection: And that is, To take their Bibles as they find them. This might ferve their turn to all intents and purpofes; were it not, that the church here interferes again; under whofe authority they muft receive them by tradition, through the feveral ages of her exiftence; as fhe affumes to be " the keeper, and wit-" nefs, of holy writ." And this unluckily makes one, in part, of her *Thirty-nine articles.*

This however is the cafe: For as the oracles of God, in the Old Teftament, were committed unto the *Jewifh* church; fo are the divine oracles of both Old, and New, committed to the care of the Chri-ftian church: Whence fhe is properly ftiled, *The pillar and ground,* or, as it is in the *margin,* the ftay, *of the truth*[c].

[c] 1 Tim. iii. 15.

This

This privilege, and this authority, is afcribed to the church, and maintained by
Calvin himfelf; for which take his own
words.—" The Lord, faith he, fo re-
" commendeth the authority of his church,
" that when it is violated, he reckons his
" own to be diminifhed. Neither is it of
" fmall importance, that the church is
" called, *The pillar, and ftay, of the truth* ;
" *and the houfe of God:* By which words
" *Paul* fignifieth, that to the end the truth
" of God fhould not fail in the world, the
" church is a faithful keeper of it ; becaufe
" God's will was to have the preaching
" of his word kept pure, by her miniftry,
" and labour; and fo to approve himfelf
" to us as the Father of his houfehold,
" while he thus feedeth us with fpiritual
" nourifhments ; and procureth all things
" that make for our falvation [f]."

In

[f] Sic ejus (ecclefiæ) authoritatem commendat (Do-
minus) ut dum illa violatur, fui ipfius imminutam cen-
feat. Neque enim parvi momenti eft, quod vocatur co-
lumna, et firmamentum veritatis, et domus Dei. Qui-
bus verbis fignificat *Paulus,* ne intercidat veritas Dei in

In a word, fubfcription to the fcriptures, in the loofe and general terms that are propofed, anfwers no other end than to profefs, we are not heathens, nor *Ma-hometans*; but that we are chriftians of fome denomination, or other.

Nor would a declaration that we are pro-teftants, much mend the matter. This hath been fpoken to already [s]. I fhall only add here, that we cannot make a more ac-ceptable compliment to the church of *Rome*, nor to the enemies of our common chriftianity, than to wave fubfcription to our articles. *If we take away the hedge of the Lord's vineyard, and break down the wall thereof; it will be laid wafte, and trodden down. The boar out of the wood will wafte it; and the wild beaft of the field will*

mundo, ecclefiam effe fidem ejus cuftodem: Quia ejus minifterio et operâ, voluit Deus puram verbi fui prædicationem confervari; et fe nobis oftendere patrem familiâs, cum nos fpiritualibus alimentis pafcit; et quæ-cunque ad falutem noftram faciunt, procurat. Calv. Inftit. lib. iv. cap. i fect. 10.

[s] P. 69.

I   *devour*

devour it. It will be open to the incurfions of all invaders; and we fhall have no fecurity againft falfe teachers of any kind.

Upon the whole, our fafety lies in our union; nor can the church of Chrift ever flourifh, or profper, while it is torn by divifions. Schifms in the church are no lefs dangerous, than factions in the ftate; and concord and unanimity are the firmeft bonds of fociety in both.

The heathen foldiers thought it a pity to rend the feamlefs coat of Chrift: And do his own difciples feel no remorfe in offering that violence, not to his garment, but to his body, the church, of which they are members?

In former times, good men, on both fides, not only lamented our divifions, and wifhed our breaches might be made up; but they ufed all their endeavours for that purpofe. No lefs than five or fix attempts were made in the laft century, to remove the fcruples of our diffenting brethren, to reconcile them to the church, and to bring about a comprehenfion. How they all,

L 2   and

and the laſt eſpecially, which was far proceeded in, came to miſcarry, is to no purpoſe now to enquire; and perhaps might
be invidious to relate.

The ill ſucceſs of theſe endeavours diſ-
couraged all future hopes of a compre-
henſion; and the number of ſects having
rather been increaſed, than diminiſhed,
ſince the revolution, ſeems to have rendered
ſuch a deſign leſs practicable. The toleration then granted is looked upon as a
ſanction to them, which gives them a
kind of eſtabliſhment.

Indeed men ſeem to have loſt all ſight
of a reconciliation of our religious differences; and the late ſtruggles which have
been made to throw off all connection with
the national church, without any firm
bond of union among the authors of them,
too plainly ſhews, what ſpirit they are
of; and that they are more diſpoſed to fly
from, than to draw towards, any one common centre: Whereby they become *enemies to the croſs of Chriſt*, and militate
againſt chriſtianity itſelf.

Perhaps

Perhaps we are all too much to blame in this refpect; and have all been too inattentive to the cultivation of that truly chriftian temper, which conciliates, and unites thofe that are poffeffed of it, to each other.

This however is certain, that we all have many great and national offences to anfwer for: And that it is *for the fins of our prophets, and the iniquities of our priefts;* as well as for the manifold tranfgreffions of the people of this land in general, which are grown to fuch an enormous height, that *the anger of the Lord hath divided us* [h]; and hath fuffered the fpirit of difcord to go forth, and prevail to fuch an alarming degree, that it is high time we fhould humble ourfelves under the mighty hand of God; and betake ourfelves to appeafe his wrath, by a national repentance and reformation; in order to prevent the infliction of feverer judgements. If we agree in nothing elfe, we fhould agree in

[h] Lam. iv. 13. 16.

L 3   this:

this: And that may in time difpofe us to be like-minded in other refpects.

As this great calamity is to be imputed to our fins in general, it concerns us all to enquire into the more immediate fources of it; not with a view of accufing, and recriminating againft, each other; but that every party, and every individual, may all call themfelves to a ftrict account, wherein, and how far, they have feverally contributed to our divifions—Whether they have taken an active part in them; or have encouraged, provoked, fomented, countenanced, or even connived at them? And whether, upon the fevereft fcrutiny, we either can acquit, or muft condemn, ourfelves, of having been any way inftrumental, in promoting, or continuing of our unhappy differences and divifions, we fhould all bear in our minds a deep fenfe of the mifchiefs of feparation; and endeavour, by all the means in our power, to guard againft, and overcome them. We fhould recollect, that difcord is an evil,

pregnant

pregnant with many evil confequences; and that neither the church of Chrift in general, nor any particular branch of it, can profper where it prevails.

As the beft means of fubduing it, we fhould all embrace *catholick and uniting principles*; which, if duly implanted, and cultivated in our minds, will operate, with a magnetick force, to attract us towards each other: I fay, *catholick* and *uniting*; and I join thofe two terms together, becaufe they are infeparable in their natures; and neither can be effectual, or complete without the other.

Univerfal benevolence is the acknowledged duty of all chriftians; and ought certainly to be extended to all thofe who differ from us in religious fentiment. This all muft allow. And therefore it is common to hear men make great profeffions of charity, towards thofe they cannot agree with in this refpect. But where interefts clafh, charity too often fuffers; and a flender acquaintance with human nature may convince us, that in a matter of fo

L 4 interefting

interefting a concern, as religion, our re-
fentment, againft fuch as differ from us in
it, generally rifes in proportion to our zeal
for it. Hence men will hardly be brought
to any true, and cordial affection towards
each other, when there are confiderable
differences in their religious principles,
opinions, modes of worfhip, and difcipline. It is next to impoffible, fo he-
terogeneous a mixture fhould be brought
to incorporate. But uniformity of worfhip naturally promotes unity of fentiment;
and unity of fentiment, unity of affection.

On the other hand, if our charity be
fincere, and truly chriftian, it will warm
our hearts towards each other; and will
draw us together *with the cords of a man,*
with the bands of love. It will difpofe
us to *a fellowfhip of fpirit* ; and by degrees
will bring us *to fpeak the fame things* ; to
profefs the fame doctrines; and to be
joined together in the fame judgement,
belief, and principle. But if men are fhy,
and fufpicious, and keep aloof from each
other—If they are ftiff, and uncomplying,
and

and are more difpofed to widen our breaches, than to clofe them; let them profefs what they will, they fhew, that a private, party fpirit ftill prevails; and that is not the fpirit of the Gofpel.

Great profeffions of charity are often met with, in the writings of the weaker party: But if they are not accompanied with fome more fubftantial proofs than words; they give room to fufpect, they are meant only to keep fair with thofe in power.

It would become all—It would be the praife of all parties, to turn their eyes, with a more favourable afpect, towards each other; and to confider, whether there be not a poffibility, if not of re-conciling our differences, yet of approach-ing nearer to each other—To that end, let not the one wait, in expectation of the other's moving firft; but let there be a laudable emulation for the lead in this refpect.

It is therefore humbly fubmitted to our governors in church and ftate, whether it would

would be at all beneath—whether it would not be worthy the dignity, and suitable to the known moderation, of the church of *England,* to make the firſt advance?

And ſurely all thoſe ſeveral bodies of proteſtants, which ſeparate from her, would be moved by the example, to take ſome ſteps to meet the national church; if they would not even contend, who ſhould appear foremoſt in ſo good a cauſe; each being aſhamed to be left behind.

As a proof of their good diſpoſitions in this reſpect, they will moderate the ſtile of their writings; ſoften all acrimony of ex-preſſion; avoid and diſcourage all inflam-matory and ſeditious diſcourſes, and pub-lications; and in their whole conduct, *follow after the things that make for peace.*

They will conſider, that not only in their ſeparate capacities each, but that all in their joint capacities likewiſe, are in-ferior in number to the church of *England*; and form the leſſer body in general: And that, as in natural and political bodies, the lighter is outweighed by the heavier, and

and attracted by it; and the weaker gives way
to the ftronger; fo in the religious world,
in this refpect, the leffer body of chriftians
fhould yield to the greater, fubmit to the
laws of attraction, and fuffer themfelves to
be drawn by the greater force, and united to
it; provided the differences between them
fhould prove to be not quite unfurmount-
able; and might be reduced within fuch
a compafs as to afford the profpect of a reconciliation: Becaufe it is a firft principle
in fociety, as obferved already, that the
inclinations of the minority be over-ruled
by the judgement and decifion of the fuperior number. And indeed it is no more
than the chriftian law of unity requires,
that they fhould conform, as far they can;
without putting a force upon their own
confciences; and that in leffer matters,
and matters otherwife of indifference at
leaft, they fhould yield fo far, as they are
indifferent; make fome compliances and
conceffions; and offer fome cheap facrifices,
that would coft them little, or nothing.

And

And would God, they would reflect, that matters of *indifference* make no inconfiderable part of the *differences* between us!

For thefe reafons, our diffenting brethren will not fcruple to agree, in making the church of *England* the *bafis* and centre of an union, or comprehenfion. The author of *The rights of the chriftian church*, feems to apprehend, that the uniting of chriftians under any one external head, or form of government, as the centre of catholick union and communion, muft inevitably terminate in a *Popedom.* But as long as the church of *England* is dependent upon the ftate, all fuch apprehenfions are as groundlefs, as, in this writer, they were affected.

The apoftle's rule, in the cafe before us, merits our moft ferious attention. *Whereto we have already attained, let us walk by the fame rule: Let us mind the fame thing* [1]. As far as we have hitherto attained, or poffibly can attain unto; or advance towards each other, let us ftrive

[1] Phil. iii. 16.

5   to

to accompany one another, walk together, and bring our fentiments, as nearly as we can, to concur with each other. And if there be ftill fome fcruples which we cannot overcome, or fome doubts and dif- ficulties, which we are not able to get over—if in any fuch things as thefe, we ftill continue to be *otherwife minded,* God, when he fees the good difpofitions of our hearts, fhall, in his due time, *reveal even this unto us* [k].

Now fuppofing an attempt to bring about a comprehenfion were determined upon; the firft thing that feems to prefent itfelf is, *a revifal of our articles and liturgy*; in whatever manner the wifdom of our go- vernors in church and ftate may think fit. And it is the heart's defire of many good, and very refpectable perfons; and many of the firmeft friends of the church of *Eng- land;* both among the clergy and laity, that this work fhould be fet about; and that fuch alterations may be made in both, as would remove all real objections, and

[k] Phil. ver. 15.

give

give all reasonable satisfaction to those that
are without, as well as within, the church.

The articles might undergo a particular
scrutiny; and be reduced to the touchstone
of scripture, one by one. The most fundamental ones, and those against popery,
I take it for granted, would, for substance,
be retained: And the speculative articles,
with such others, as are of less confequence, might be omitted, or altered, as
would be judged most proper: And some
respecting the present times might perhaps
be inserted in their stead. But that, upon
the whole, the number of them should
be rather reduced, than added to; that *no
greater burden be laid* upon subscribers, than
what consists of *necessary things;* according
to the apostolical rule [1].

As no human composition is so perfect,
as not to be capable of improvement; and
as there is no antient composition in our
language, but what must suffer particu-

[1] Acts xv. 28.

larly,

larly, by the mutation and flux of it; and though perhaps nothing hath contributed more to the prefervation of the*Englifh* language, than the conftant ufe of our liturgy, and of the fcriptures, in the vulgar tongue; yet, I prefume, no one now doubts, but that the liturgy may be improved; by the change of obfolete words, phrafes, and cuftoms—by fome more fubftantial alterations in its fervice—by the addition, perhaps, of fome occafional offices—and by the better adjufting of fome circumftantials of external order.

And I flatter myfelf that when the trial comes to be made, there will not be much need of improvement found, befides in circumftantials. Our church is found in its conftitution; and I truft feels no decay in its integral parts, that wants much, if any, repair. But if whatever improvements it is capable of, in doctrine, difcipline, and worfhip, were made in it, confiftently with the fundamentals of chriftianity, and the principles on which

it

it is eftablifhed [m]; the benefits would be manifold, and ineftimable.

This would enlarge the borders of our church—would conciliate fome to her—would filence others; and give no juft caufe of offence to any. It would, at the fame time, be highly beneficial to ourfelves. It would be the means of our greater edification, and would render our liturgy ftill the more *reafonable fervice.* It would demonftrate our candor and ingenuity—would teftify our charity, and defire to embrace all thofe that feparate from us. It would juftify our conduct to the world: It would be an additional recommendation of our church, to all other proteftant churches; and, if brought to a

---

[m] *Tertullian* lays down an excellent rule in this refpect. Regula quidem fidei una omnino eft, fola immobilis, et irreformabilis, credendi fcilicet in unicum Deum—et filium ejus Jefum Chriftum—Hâc lege fidei manente, cætera jam difciplinæ, et converfationis, admittunt novitatem correctionis, operante fcilicet, et proficiente ufque ad finem gratiâ Dei.

Tertull. de virg. velandis, cap. 1.

happy

happy conclufion, would be the glory of the prefent reign.

As chriftians, in their private capacities, ought always to be going on unto perfection; fo ought they, in their publick and aggregate capacity, the church, likewife.

" It is the glory of our *Englifh church,*" fays one of her learned divines, " and " what fhe often boafts of, that fhe is the " *nearefl* of any now in the chriftian " world, to the primitive model. It is " not, I prefume, denied, that fhe might " be *nearer* ftill: And if her glory be " great, for being fo *near*; it would cer- " tainly be greater, if fhe were yet " *nearer*[n]."

In purfuance of this noble defign, I beg leave to hint at one or two improvements more in our church; which fome time or other, it may be prefumed, will take place.

[n] Dr. *Marfhal's* preface to his tranflation of St. *Cyprian*, p. 12.

M   Though

Though our *Englifh* tranflation of the Bible is an excellent one; and, in the judgement of a very learned man, the beft in the world[o]; yet it is thought to have its imperfections; and a new tranflation hath been long wifhed for, as one of our greateft *defiderata.* The diftribution of this undertaking among feveral able hands, in like manner with that, in which the laft tranflation, made by authority, was executed, would render this great work the more eafy, expeditious, and accurate : And the original languages of holy writ having of late been much ftudied; it cannot be faid we are in want of perfons duly qualified for the tafk.

An excellent body of laws [p] was drawn up, for the ufe of our church, at the beginning of the Reformation ; but, unhappily, it could never obtain the fanction of publick authority ; and it hath ever fince lain dormant, as a dead letter. If the times would bear, that thefe laws, and our

---

[o] Mr. *Selden,* in his Table Talk.

[p] *Reformatio legum ecclefiafticarum.*

2   canons.

canons too, might be revifed, and enforced by the authority of the legiflature; nothing would be more defirable, if any thing more could be defired, for the improvement of our difcipline.

Bifhop *Burnet* hints, that the Reformation was not carried on to the perfection, that was defigned, and wifhed for; and he exhorts us to wait, and pray for fuch a glorious conjuncture, as may reftore every thing among us to a primitive purity and fplendor ᵠ. We have waited long; and I doubt we have long to wait ftill, before the whole of fo large a defign be carried into execution. However, we may do fomething towards it—fomething might be attempted towards making a beginning. We at leaft may, and ought to make it the fubject of our conftant, and fervent prayers: Nor do I fee, that the prefent conjuncture is fo unfavourable for it, as many, I doubt, apprehend it to be. The prejudices of fome churchmen, to which the mifcarriage of a comprehenfion,

ᵠ Conclufion of his Hiftory of the Reformation.

M 2   defigned

defigned in 1689, hath been chiefly imputed, are now entirely worn away. We may learn wifdom from the hiftory of it. The proceedings in that defign are known to be extant; and recourfe, I prefume, may be had to them. They may ferve as a good ground-work to build upon : And the voice of the publick calls for the tryal. And if it be fet about in good earneft, our church, under the divine *aufpices*, may be brought to a re-femblance of the purity and fimplicity of the primitive church; and our *Zion* may become the *joy of the whole earth.* It may by degrees draw near to that perfect ftate, which we have grounds to hope the uni-verfal church will at length arrive at; when Chrift, her fpoufe, fhall *prefent her to himfelf a glorious church, not having fpot, or wrinkle, or any fuch thing; being holy, and without blemifh.*

To conclude. We have feen, that there is fuch a thing, as to be perfectly joined together, *in the fame mind, and in the fame judgement*; otherwife, we would not be exhorted to it. We would not be fo much

intreated

intreated, and preſſed, to endeavour at what is impoſſible to be attained ; nor en-couraged to hope for ſuch happineſs, as is never to be acquired.

Such divines therefore muſt ſurely have but ill learned Chriſt, or muſt have loſt all ſight of his precepts, who pronounce " any " attempt towards avoiding diverſity of " opinion to be not only an *uſeleſs,* but an " *impracticable* ſcheme ʳ." What ! are our religious *differences* ſuch *indifferent* things, that it is immaterial what our opinions are ? Is it of no uſe to avoid, or prevent, perſecutions, and maſſacres, which have often been the conſequences of them ? And is the peace and harmony of the Chri-ſtian world not worth preſerving ? · And to pronounce that to be impracticable, which God, in his holy word, hath en-joined, and declared to be attainable, is ſtrange divinity indeed.

However diſcouraging the proſpect may be at preſent, we are aſſured, by the higheſt authority, and by the certainty of

ʳ Confeſſional, p. 2,

· M 3   fact,

fact, that a perfect harmony once reigned in the church of Chrift. The firft difciples were *all of one heart, and one foul:* And we have good grounds to hope, that the fame bleffed temper fhall again prevail among Chriftians. The prophet *Ezekiel* foretels, that the *two fticks,* of *Judah* and *Jofeph,* fhall in the end be joined together, and *become one;* and the whole houfe of *Ifrael* be *one nation*—that they *all fhall have one fhepherd;* and that *one king fhall be king over them all*[s].

And to prevent all doubt, whether this concerns the chriftian church, our Saviour himfelf affures us, that it likewife in the end fhall confift of *one fold, and one fhepherd*[t]. Not to cite any other predictions, and prophetical intimations of the fame bleffed event.

We have good grounds therefore to hope, that the time will come, when we of this nation, notwithftanding prefent appearances, fhall have our breaches repaired, and become *one fold* likewife, and

---

[s] Ezek. xxxvii. 15—24.   [t] John x. 16.

be

be gathered into one body, under the good
fhepherd of our fouls; who gave his life
for the fheep, that he might unite them
to himfelf, and to each other. We will,
therefore beware of defeating the end of
his death by our divifions.

Our Lord reprefents his church under
the lively emblem of a *vine*, of which he
reckons himfelf to be the root; and the
members of it as the branches; which
therefore can have no life, but what they
draw from him. He teaches them, that,
by their abiding in him, they bear fruit,
and flourifh; but, if they abide not in
him, he moft affuredly warns them of
their wretched fate; which can be none
other, than to be rejected, as withered
branches; which are fit for nothing, but
to be *caft into the fire, and burned* u.

We have feen, that our Saviour confiders us all, as one body, and himfelf, as
the head of it. What a grievous thing is
it, for the members to raife a mutiny in
this body! How muft they all fuffer by it!

u John xvi. 1—6.

M 4   And

And how dreadful the consequence in the end, if continued in! How necessary therefore is it to our mutual preservation, that it be appeased!

The apostle intreats us, to use all our endeavours *to keep the unity of the Spirit in the bond of peace* ; and enforces his advice with various arguments, to the same purpose. Shall we be deaf to them all? Nor suffer them to have any weight with us? We have seen, that by unity in the faith it is, that the body of Christ is to be edified. By disunion then it must be destroyed.

This great principle of unity is the chief cement, by which this his whole body is fitly and closely compacted together, diffusing itself, and efficaciously pervading every part ; promoting the increase and edification of the whole, in love. Surely, it is very unnatural to aim at dissolving this cement, so essential to our own subsistence—to offer at untying, much more at cutting, this sacred knot, in which all

all our ſtrength lieth. On the contrary, we ſhould think it incumbent upon us— we ſhould think it our mutual intereſt, one and all, to conſpire, in drawing it cloſer, if we poſſibly can—in improving; and in the end, perfecting ourſelves in love: By which means, we ſhall attain unto the original ſtandard of our nature—*unto the full meaſure, and ſtature of Chriſt.*

Therefore, *If there be any conſolation in Chriſt—If any comfort of love—If any fellowſhip of the Spirit—If any bowels and mercies; fulfill ye our* common *joy; that ye be like-minded, having the ſame love, being of one accord, of one mind*[w]*. And put on, as the elect of God, holy and beloved, bowels of mercies, kindneſs, humbleneſs of mind, meekneſs, long-ſuffering, forbearing one another. And, above all things, put on charity; which is the bond of perfectneſs; and let the peace of God rule in your hearts; to which alſo ye are called in one body*[x],

---

[w] Phil. ii. 1, 2.
[x] Col. iii. 12—15.

And

And the God of patience and confolation grant you to be like-minded one towards another, according to Chrift Jefus: That ye may, with one mind, and one mouth, glorify God, even the Father of our Lord Jefus Chrift[y], Amen.

I cannot better clofe thefe papers, than with the following prayer, taken out of our excellent liturgy; which deferves to be oftener ufed in our publick worfhip.

" O God, the Father of our Lord Jefus
" Chrift, our only Saviour, the Prince of
" Peace! give us grace ferioufly to lay to
" heart the great dangers we are in, by
" our unhappy divifions. Take away all
" hatred and prejudice, and whatfoever
" elfe may hinder us from godly union,
" and concord: That, as there is but one
" body; and one Spirit; and one hope
" of our calling; one Lord; one faith;
" one baptifm; one God and Father of
" us all: So we may henceforth be all
" of one heart, and of one foul; united
" in one holy bond, of truth and peace,

[y] Rom, xv. 5, 6.

" of

" of faith and charity; and may with
" one mind, and one mouth, glorify
" thee, through Jefus Chrift our Lord.
" Amen ᶻ."

ᶻ From the Office for the King's Acceſſion to
the Throne.

The E N D,